SEEK OUT THE WAY

Books of Interest

Light on the Path
and an Essay on Karma

The Idyll of the White Lotus
Mabel Collins

The Creative Silence — Reflections on
The Voice of the Silence

The Eternal Light
Rohit Mehta

Talks on the Path of Occultism
(Vol. III – Commentary on *Light on the Path*)
Annie Besant and C. W. Leadbeater

The Technique of the Spiritual Life
Clara M. Codd

SEEK OUT THE WAY

(Studies in *Light on the Path*)

ROHIT MEHTA

THE THEOSOPHICAL PUBLISHING HOUSE
Adyar, Chennai 600 020, India • Wheaton, IL, USA

© The Theosophical
Publishing House, 1955

Second Edition, Second Reprint 2007

ISBN 81-7059-513-4 (Hard Cover)
ISBN 81-7059-146-5 (Soft Cover)

Printed at the Vasanta Press
The Theosophical Society
Adyar, Chennai, 600 020, India

Cover design: Sushama Sreenath

Contents

1. The Raging of the Storm — 1
2. The State of Aloneness — 15
3. Surrender to the Unknown — 33
4. The Discovery of the Path — 49
5. The Fighter and the Warrior — 63
6. The Creative Silence — 80
7. The Whisper of the Soul — 91
8. The Three Inquiries — 101
9. The Middle Way — 111

Preface

Light on the Path is one of the most precious gems in the literature of modern Theosophy. It may be described as the most outstanding book on the Mysticism of Theosophy. Ever since its publication seventy years ago, it has been a source of inspiration to large numbers of people throughout the world.

The origins of this book have been 'lost in the mists of prehistoric antiquity', and in the course of several thousand years its form has been enlarged by the inclusion of different commentaries. In its original form it is believed to have contained thirty aphorisms written as a palm-leaf manuscript. These have been retained in the modern editions of the book, but together with the commentaries and notes that have been added, in its present form the book is much larger than it was in ancient times. The aphorisms contain spiritual instructions of profound significance.

A book like *Light on the Path* transcends all limitations of age and race and, therefore, has universal application. The instructions it contains are of as great value to the men and women of our time as they were to the spiritual aspirants of previous generations.

Like all great spiritual treatises, *Light on the Path* contains several layers of meaning. I have attempted, in these pages, to present that meaning which has most appealed to me. As one grows in understanding one discovers new layers of meaning in this deeply penetrating book of Theosophical Mysticism.

The title of this book, *Seek Out the Way*, has been selected from the text itself. It is one of the shortest of the aphorisms appearing in *Light on the Path*, and the entire text is, as it were, woven round this instruction of four words. The book has grown out of a series of talks given to a group of students at the Indian Section Headquarters of the Theosophical Society in Banaras (now Vārānasi).

ROHIT MEHTA

17 November 1955

1

The Raging of the Storm

One of the most baffling problems in living a spiritual life is to sustain one's interest and enthusiasm in the midst of endless difficulties and the severest trials. The routine and monotony of everyday existence sap one's vitality and strength. The lives of most people are made up of small events and incidents — what one might call the trivialities of existence. Great and extraordinary events occur but rarely in the lives of average men and women. To show enthusiasm for extraordinary things is easy, but to maintain it in the midst of daily routine is extremely difficult. The greatest trial consists in maintaining a spiritual integrity in the midst of the common details of life. To maintain a perfect balance of thought and emotion in the midst of the ceaseless provocations of daily existence demands a strength which most men are unable to display. And yet the test of man's spiritual life lies in the field of ordinary activities, not in the spheres of extraordinary achievements.

Emerson said that nothing great was ever achieved without enthusiasm. If this be true then enthusiasm is one of the essential qualities required on the spiritual path. Without enthusiasm the path would seem tiresome. That this is so is evidenced from the lives of countless spiritual aspirants who have returned to mundane existence because of their inability to maintain enthusiasm on the path.

Now enthusiasm should not be confused with efficient discharge of one's duties. The so-called efficiency of the world is mostly due to the cultivation of certain habits. An efficient life is not necessarily creative — it is very often mechanical. A machine is efficient, but it is not enthusiastic. It carries out its duties in a flawless manner, but one cannot associate an element of joy with what the machine does. An enthusiastic life, however, has creativity in it. Its actions are not stereotyped but bear an individuality of their own.

Enthusiasm for anything arises from a condition of deep interest. Once again enthusiasm should not be confused with mere excitement. An excitement has no depth in it, and therefore, it cannot sustain itself. It needs to be constantly fed by the sensations of the outer world. But enthusiasm rooted in deep interest draws its sustenance from that very depth. The mind that is capable of deep interest knows no moment of dullness and is never deterred by obstacles, however great they may be.

The difficulty with most of us is that we live at a very superficial level — our thoughts and emotions are extremely shallow. This tendency towards superficiality has greatly increased in recent times because of an undue emphasis on speed. Our civilization is in a state of terrific hurry — although it does not know where it is hurrying to! A superficial life is in constant need of excitement, materially or spiritually. There is a craving for more and more excitement, sensation, entertainment. This demand for more is seen at all levels of man's existence. Needless to say, a mind which functions at superficial levels can have no deep experiences. Such a mind has only acquaintances, but no deep friendships. It can dissect and analyse a structure, but it cannot comprehend the depths of the indwelling Life. Spirituality is essentially a matter of deep experience. It is the depth of experience which characterizes spirituality and not a particular field of activity. One may be intensely spiritual in the marketplace — and another may not be spiritual at all even while dwelling all the time in a temple or a shrine.

It is the person living in the shallows who quarrels with the objective conditions of life. He moves with a sense of injustice, has a sense of grievance against the Lords of Karma and feels thwarted by the circumstances in which he has been placed. The surface of water is constantly whipped up by the passing wind. Does man struggle to be secure from these constant disturbances by trying to control the wind? To strive for security by attempting to alter the objective conditions of life displays an immature mind. A mind, devoid of depth, feels restricted by the objective environment, be it of things, persons or ideas. When the mind's contact with life is shallow and superficial the difficulties of the objective world loom very large.

Kabir, a great Indian mystic, says that when deep sleep does not come to the eyes a person makes a great fuss about the making of the bed and the arranging of the pillows. It is only the dancer who has no dance within her who complains about the stage, the floor and the make-up. When the life within has dried up objective difficulties seem insurmountable. A lack of deep interest slows down man's enthusiasm. He who is dried up within seeks renewal from without! Yet, no change in the objective condition, no alteration in the setting of Karma will bring renewal to he who does not enter the very depths of his own being.

Is it possible for man to cultivate a deep interest for life? Can such an interest be created at all — or is it only a gift of Karma? Is spiritual life a matter of mere subjectivism denying all reality in objective conditions? Has the spiritual man not to work at changing objective circumstances?

Objective conditions are meant to serve as fields of expression for man. Therefore, they do need to be changed and altered from time to time that they may not cause any restriction on man's expressional urges. Objective circumstances, in other words, are instruments of expression. One may alter an instrument, perhaps decorate it, but if there is no music within the heart, of what use will that instrument be? Music in the heart must precede all the activities of changing and polishing the instrument.

The change in objective conditions must follow — not precede — the arousing of deep interest. If we expect that interest will be aroused as a result of objective changes then we are utterly mistaken. We may be put in a new setting by the Lords of Karma, but if the mind is dull and insensitive it will not see the beauties of the new environment. If there is deep interest, changes, if needed, in the objective environment, will be brought about in a smooth and silent manner. Even if the setting cannot be changed, the man of deep interest and enthusiasm will put new life and vitality into the old forms of environment. When there is dance within, the dancer can dance anywhere and impart a freshness to an erstwhile dull and drab setting. Is this not what a poet does with the language that is given to him?

The experience of all spiritual mystics is that objective difficulties are swept away under the impact of enthusiasm born of deep interest. Enthusiasm and deep interest are a joint phenomenon, or to put it differently, one is the expression while the other is the source. Enthusiasm arises only in a state of deep interest intrinsically present — not relatively, but absolutely present — in the subject. It means that the interest is not about something; it is not in relation to a particular thing. The state of pure interest alone serves as a ground for real enthusiasm. Interest in *something* only produces superficiality because it serves as a tether to the mind. A sensitivity merely to something is no sensitivity at all for by the unconscious process of resistance it makes the mind insensitive to other things. A mind that is open only to some particular thing is a closed mind. The condition of pure interest is essential for the awakening of enthusiasm.

The mind that has enormous space in it is capable of deep interest. The mind that has no space is a shallow or a superficial mind. To have space is to possess a depth in which to receive and retain the influences and the impulses of life. A shallow mind receives little and therefore gives to life also, very little. When the receiving is shallow, the giving too is meagre, devoid of all generosity.

Is it possible for one to create a depth in the mind? The lack of depth is indeed the main subjective difficulty, causing the objective handicaps to loom very large. There may be an objective heaven but without a subjective depth it will be of no use. The influences of that heaven cannot pour their richness into a mind that is shallow. The practical problem for all spiritual aspirants is, therefore, the creation of this depth or space in the mind. How can the influences of the Master or Truth pour into a mind that has no space in it? If a space could be created in the mind, then one's life will have deep moments of experience everyday. Even daily routine and the small details of life will take on a significance, irradiated with a new light. They will become the stream and the rivulets, bringing rich treasures to be poured into the sea. The sea with its enormous depth will contain them all — and more.

How is this space to be created in the mind so that its contacts with life may be deep and abiding? One should remember that it is not by merely increasing one's points of contact with life that this depth can be created. Not by a quantitative approach but only by a qualitative transformation can a deep contact with life become possible.

To create space in the mind is to have a mind that has no resisting element in it, whether at the conscious or at the unconscious level. If the mind resists, it will lose its pliability and therefore become insensitive. In order to understand the depth of the mind, one must observe the deep silence that descends in Nature after a heavy storm. This silence can be experienced on the mountain tops or in deep valleys, near the sea or on the plains. When the storm rages it appears as if everything will be destroyed under its overwhelming spell. And yet, after the storm there is to be seen a complete cleansing in Nature — a purification of the atmosphere — a freshness and a silence that is deep and vibrant. The dead leaves and the branches are swept away and it appears as if a complete renewal of Nature has taken place. *Light on the Path* says:

> Look for the flower to bloom in the silence that follows the storm; not till then.

> It shall grow, it will shoot up, it will make branches and leaves and form buds while the storm continues, while the battle lasts. But not till the whole personality of the man is dissolved and melted — not until it is held by the divine fragment which has created it, as a mere subject for grave experiment and experience — not until the whole nature has yielded and become subject unto its Higher Self, can the bloom open.

The opening of the bloom is the deep spiritual experience which comes after the terrific raging of the storm. It is in the storm that the depth of silence is created. The cleansing of Nature by the storm is indeed the creation of space. The silence that follows the storm is most significant. The storm so deeply stirs Nature that all dead things are cast off and the burden of the past is swept away.

Similarly, the mind of man can be renewed only if the burden of its past is carried away and it is rendered lighter and pliable. Deep silence can come to the mind provided it can be deeply stirred. A mind that is placid, indifferent, casual, unmoved, can never experience the depths and therefore cannot know what renewal is. Such a mind can be excited but not enthused. A capacity to be stirred, disturbed, is a necessary precondition for the arousing of interest and enthusiasm. If nothing disturbs a man, then there is something fundamentally wrong with him! Fortunately there is something or other which does disturb us. This is the saving grace of our life! It shows that we are not dead although we may be asleep.

However if disturbances do come into our lives

and if storms rage within us, why do they not create depths in our consciousness? Why do they not cleanse our minds? Why are we not renewed after mental and emotional storms? This is because we resist the storms. We interfere with their movements, we want to control them. We are afraid of allowing the storm to work itself through us. We feel we will be destroyed under its impact; we feel we will be swept away under its fearful sway. Therefore, when these psychological storms rage within us, we resist their arrival, and when they come we try to make our way through them.

To try to push one's way through a storm or a disturbance is fraught with grave dangers. When a storm rages one is confused. If the confusion is not there, then the storm too is not there! During a storm there is the raising of dust and the shaking up of trees and plants. One is naturally confused in the midst of this upheaval, and so whatever steps one takes in this moment of confusion is bound to lead one to greater confusion. In storms and disturbances one must 'stay put', as every movement of the confused mind is likely to lead the spiritual pilgrim astray. If the storm is allowed to work itself out — and if no resistance is put before it — then there will be a complete cleansing of the mind. The mind will be refreshed and renewed. A new way and a new approach will open out before such a mind. And a new way always calls out enthusiasm from within the heart of each man.

But the question is: Are we to invite storms and disturbances in order to create enthusiasm for life? The remedy seems to be worse than the disease! What after all is a storm or a disturbance? It is obviously a challenge from life. We are disturbed by these challenges. But consider — since in the river of life new waters flow through every moment, life is a never-ceasing challenge. There is no moment when life's challenge does not exist. Why do we not find ourselves in a state of alertness, although challenges should make a man alert and vigilant? If we are surrounded by challenges and if we are not alert and vigilant, are we not sheltering ourselves under a false security?

There is no doubt that life sends out constantly, never-ceasingly, challenges from all sides and at various levels. But the mind, through the responses that emanate from its spheres of memory, works as a 'shock-absorber' to these challenges. This intervening activity of the mind lulls us to sleep, and prevents us from meeting the challenges of life. The mind is interested in acting as an intermediary because thus alone can it maintain its continuity. We do not even become aware of the challenges. Yet, sometimes the fortifications of the mind collapse because of the overwhelming nature of the challenge — but such instances come rarely in the life of an ordinary man. Mostly, he is unaware of the challenges of life that arise from moment to moment because of the screen which his mind places between him and his environment. The mind keeps him away from a direct contact with life. It is to a stagnant existence that most of us are committed. How can there be enthusiasm in such a stagnant existence?

If the mind could receive the challenges of life without sending out any response from its centres of memory, it would remain fresh and vital. Even as Nature is cleansed by the storms that rage, so will the mind of man be cleansed by the challenges of life. To receive life's challenges but not to react to them from the centres of memory is to 'stay put' in the midst of a storm — it is to stand still where one is; for any movement by the mind in the hour of storm would lead the spiritual pilgrim to greater and greater confusion.

To stand still in a storm requires tremendous

courage. Not to resist the storm or to run away from it implies receiving its full impact. And in receiving the impact man is rendered absolutely alone. Challenge without response is a state of aloneness. When a storm rages in Nature every tree is alone, for it has to rely on its own strength. In that aloneness, if the tree does not resist, it becomes lighter with the shedding away of dead leaves and branches. Similarly, if man could stand still, alone in the storm, he will find himself completely renewed. In subjective renewal, the difficulties of the objective environment vanish as into thin air. The aloneness created by the storm is fraught with tremendous spiritual possibilities. It is to these that we shall turn as we consider the problem of aloneness in the next chapter.

2

The State of Aloneness

Plotinus very picturesquely described the path of spiritual realization as a 'flight of the alone to the Alone'. This element of 'aloneness' has been stressed with reference to spiritual life by the mystics of all ages. *Light on the Path*, too, exhorts the disciple to 'stand alone'. The spiritual journey has to be undertaken in absolute aloneness, for the Path to Reality is so narrow that there is space for only one to walk at a time. The great Indian mystic, Kabir, says in one of his famous songs: 'The Path of Love is so narrow that on it there is no place for two.'

One can understand the aloneness of the spiritual pilgrim owing to the narrowness of the path, but why has the end of the journey, too, been described as 'Alone' by Plotinus. In the philosophical literature of the world, Reality and Absolute are synonymous. In the philosophy of the Vedānta, the Absolute is termed as Brahman, and the description of Brahman given therein is, 'One without a second'. If the Absolute or Brahman is 'One without a second' surely it stands alone. Since there is no second to it, it cannot be compared to or contrasted with anything else. Thus, nothing can be more in a state of 'aloneness' than the Absolute or the Brahman. The Absolute transcends all realms of relativity for there is nothing like it — nor is there anything contrary to it. Relationship implies comparison or contrast; in fact relationship has no existence outside of these two processes. Thus spiritual pilgrimage is characterized by 'aloneness', both at the beginning as well as at the end. It indicates that it is only the alone that can move towards the Alone. It establishes the truth of the old Occult maxim which says: 'Thou canst not tread the path until thou hast become one with it.' In order to journey to the Alone, one must start in a condition of absolute aloneness. It is only the alone that will be able to comprehend the Alone.

Light on the Path says: 'To ask is to feel the hunger within.' In spiritual life this is the only asking that is recognized — all else is mere curiosity. Only when the asking arises from the

The State of Aloneness

hunger within is there a depth to it. In a superficial contact with life no spiritual realization is ever possible. We have been assured: 'Ask and it shall be given' — but the asking must come from the depths of experience. And the depth of experience is possible only in aloneness, for in that state the subject and the object face each other with nothing to disturb or distract them. How can there be a depth of experience when the mind of man is distracted in all directions? How can Truth, God or a Master enter his life, if he is not alone but is subjected to numerous distractions? The man of distractions will not even recognize the presence of God or Truth if he is not alone. The exquisite thrill of the Great Presence of Truth, God or the Master will be felt by us only in moments of absolute aloneness.

But it is this aloneness which man ever wants to escape. He is afraid of being alone and that is why he is always with somebody or something. If there is nothing on hand, no subject or object with which to occupy his mind, he digs out something through curiosity and inquisitiveness so that he may not have to face aloneness.

What is this aloneness and why is man afraid of it? Are we alone when we are just by ourselves?

Does aloneness mean avoiding other people's company? Are we alone when we refuse to talk with anybody? There is a great deal of difference between aloneness and isolation. The moments when we avoid other people's company, or the moments when we are by ourselves, not inclined to talk with anybody, may be moments of isolation but not necessarily of aloneness. In moments of isolation we are in the company of our own thoughts; in fact the company of our own thoughts is most intense and intimate in moments of isolation. How can there be aloneness when we are in the company of something?

Aloneness is not a physical condition — it is a state of the mind. The more we crave for conditions of physical isolation, the further we are from aloneness. It is not suggested here that physical isolation and aloneness are contradictory. All that is indicated here is that they do not necessarily go together. One may be utterly alone in moments of physical isolation or one may not be alone at all even though one may be completely isolated with reference to physical influences. Aloneness is a state in which the mind has nothing to hold on to. As long as it can hold on to something — an idea, an ideal, a concept, an

The State of Aloneness

image — there is no aloneness. *Light on the Path* describes this state when it asks the spiritual pilgrim to hold fast to that which has neither substance nor existence. When the mind has neither substance nor existence to hold on to, the state of aloneness is experienced.

We value most that which we receive in aloneness. We cherish it as the great prize of life. That which comes to us when we are alone is indeed of the greatest significance to us. What comes to us when we are surrounded by others or when we are in the company of our own thoughts has very little significance for us. What purpose would be served by the arrival of Truth, God or the Master in our life if we are not alone? Even the highest Truth or the sublimest Beauty would be of little significance when the experience of aloneness is absent. A thought, an idea, a vision that descends upon us in aloneness enters our very being, for there is nothing to resist or distort it. The experience that comes in aloneness has a profound revolutionary import.

If we have not experienced the compelling power of Truth it is because we have not known what aloneness is. If our contacts with life are superficial it is because we have never been alone.

Our receiving of life has no depth — it is casual. How can our giving be rich when our receiving is so poor?

This state of aloneness has been indicated in the first four sentences of *Light on the Path* and the subject of aloneness forms the main theme of this book. Aloneness, being the critical state of the mind, provides the ground in which the spiritual plant can grow. Creativity of the spirit is possible only in this aloneness. Spiritual enlightenment can come to man only when he is alone. Since *Light on the Path* deals with the problems of spiritual life it emphasizes the value and significance of aloneness.

Spiritual life is not a continuity — not even a modified continuity — of temporal life. The principle of gradualness operates in the realm of continuity. But since spiritual life indicates a new quality of existence it is not the principle of gradualness, but suddenness, that operates here. Suddenness is possible only in a critical state. In scientific terminology, a critical point is a point of transition. The mind in a state of aloneness is indeed poised at this critical point — the point of psychological or spiritual transition. At this point of transition true spiritual transformation occurs

The State of Aloneness 21

— this is indeed the Revolution at the Centre — the sudden arrival of a new quality of existence. *Light on the Path* describes this as 'the mysterious event'. It is no exaggeration to say that the central idea of that precious book is the occurrence of this 'mysterious event'. Indeed, the following passage appearing in the book holds the key to the understanding of the entire spiritual problem so beautifully and clearly discussed in its pages:

> Then will come a calm such as comes in a tropical country after the heavy rain, when Nature works so swiftly that one may see her action. Such a calm will come to the harassed spirit. And in the deep silence the mysterious event will occur which will prove that the way has been found.

The swift action of Nature is indeed the sudden appearance of a new order of existence. According to *Light on the Path* this mysterious event occurs only in deep silence — the silence that descends after a heavy storm.

It is to this deep silence, the critical state or the moment of aloneness, that the attention of the neophyte is drawn in the first four opening sentences of this great book of Mysticism. The book opens with the following instruction:

Before the eyes can see they must be incapable of tears.

When do tears come to one's eyes? When one does not like a particular situation. It means one wants things and situations to be other than what they are. When a man is unwilling to accept things and situations as they are and feels frustrated in his efforts to change them, tears come to his eyes. The tears obviously imply a loss of perspective and therefore a distortion of vision. Does not aloneness suggest looking at things and situations as they are? The eyes are capable of tears when the mind is in conflict between *what is* and *what it would like it to be*. The mind that is in the company of its own thoughts and ambitions is not in a state of aloneness. To be incapable of tears is to be willing to look at life as it is.

It must be remembered that *Light on the Path* does not suggest insensitivity of the eyes. It is true that tears can be prevented by refusing to see, by closing the eyes, by running away from a situation. But that is not the instruction given in the book. The injunction to the neophyte is: the eyes must see and yet they must be incapable of

The State of Aloneness

tears. In fact this first instruction to the spiritual pilgrim says that the eyes will not be able to see clearly so long as it is capable of tears. And tears come because of the mind's unwillingness to look at life as it is. Thus, unless the mind is alone, free from its own ambitions and affiliations, it is not possible for the neophyte to fulfil the first instruction. Usually our minds are either too dull or too interfering. If the neophyte has dulled his mind, the eyes will be incapable of seeing anything. If his mind interferes, owing to its own ambitions, refusing to accept a situation as it is, then surely fears will constantly well up, out of the conflict between what is and what the mind would like it to be. The first instruction, therefore, indicates the state of aloneness where the mind is completely free from all psychological attachments and affiliations, where it is not in the company even of its own modes or trends of thinking. It is in a condition where the 'thinking faculty is tense and yet not thinking'. To be able to see and yet be incapable of tears is indeed a state of great tension — a condition in which the mind has come to a critical point.

The second instruction given to the neophyte is:

Before the ear can hear it must have lost its sensitiveness.

How can one hear if the ears are not sensitive? Just as the first instruction does not suggest loss of sight, similarly the second instruction does not indicate loss of hearing. The word 'sensitiveness' here has a psychological — not a physical — meaning. In other words, the instruction refers to the touchiness of the mind. The fact is that it is not the ear but the mind that hears. Only when the mind ceases to be touchy can there arise the possibility of right hearing.

What does the touchiness of the mind indicate? It suggests that the mind wants to hear something other than what it does. The mind does not want to accept life as it comes through the sense of hearing. It wants life to be different. It wants to hear only that which is pleasant and avoid that which it declares to be unpleasant. The distinction of 'pleasant' and 'unpleasant' springs from the memory of past experiences. And so the touchiness of the mind arises from, and is rooted in, the past. Most of our hearing, in which the ears have not lost their sensitiveness or touchiness, is only chronologically in the present; but psychologically it is in the past. We hear only the voices of the past caught up in our mind as a memory of the pleasant and the unpleasant. Only when hearing, both physical and psychological, takes place in the present is there right hearing. Once again, to hear without a reaction from the mind is a condition of extreme tenseness comparable to a state of aloneness. When all the voices of the past are silenced, then the mind is without any company. It stands alone in complete silence. And it is only the silent that can hear. Thus, it is absolutely true that 'before the ear can hear' all reactions of the mind born out of psychological memory must cease. Only when the mind is alone can there be true hearing — this indeed is the ear losing its sensitiveness.

The third instruction given to the neophyte in the very beginning of the book is:

Before the voice can speak in the presence of the Masters it must have lost the power to wound.

Speech is one of the most powerful instruments in the hands of man. He can heal or harm others with this weapon that he possesses. Very often our speech contains a conscious or an unconscious sting. The sting of our speech is not in the word; it is undoubtedly in the mind. The word by itself has neither healing nor harming power. The thing that is conveyed through the word makes it pleasant or unpleasant. Word or language is only a form. It is the mind that imparts quality to it. Speech is a means of communication. Without it social relationship would become well-nigh impossible. But a means of communication by itself has no significance. That which is communicated makes the word or language significant. All of us use the same words and follow the same forms of language, and yet there is a distinct difference in the quality that is conveyed by each. Very often our spoken word has no power or vitality in it, but sometimes the word becomes intensely alive. Just a word from our friend many a time heals the wound from which we have been suffering, but at other times a word from the same friend deepens the wound. Why does this happen? It is not the word that matters — it is the source from which the word emerges that is of fundamental importance. The healing or the harming quality of the word resides in the source and not in the form or pattern of language.

In our day-to-day relationship with others the

source of our speech is in the mind which is conditioned by the memory of past experiences. In other words, the conditioned background of the mind is the source from where all our words emerge.

'In the beginning was the Word', says the Christian scripture. In Hinduism there is the concept of *Śabda-Brahman* — creation arising from the Word. 'As above, so below', is the age-old maxim. It indicates that what is true at the macrocosmic level is true at the microcosmic level also. Thus, the world of man arises from the word even as the macrocosmic world has arisen from the Word of God. Our world centres round the words that we use. To be able to utter a word with reference to a thing, a person, or a situation is indeed a great power. Having spoken the word man weaves his own world round about it. The uttering of a word is the act of naming an object, a person or a situation. A man does not feel that a thing is in his grip as long as he has not named it. Once an experience is named he feels utterly secure.

An experience contributes a challenge as long as man has not named it. An unnamed object or experience requires his close and undistracted attention. It is out of a desire for security that man shows eagerness to name an object or a situation. Now it is true that without naming, social life would become impossible. Naming brings order in this otherwise chaotic existence. Names are necessary for social communication. They help us to differentiate one thing from another. But verbal differentiation is one thing while psychological distinction is quite another. The names that are given to objects and situations do not merely serve the purposes of verbal location or differentiation — they stand primarily for psychological identification. In names are stored up all our psychological associations or memories. Thus to verbal differentiation we add this factor of psychological association. So when a word is uttered or a name is pronounced, there is the whole background of past associations or memories present. This background becomes the source of our speech. In other words, our speech arises from the mind that is conditioned by past associations and memories.

We rarely utter a pure word or pronounce a pure name. Our words and names are contaminated by a touch of the past. This contamination gives a sting to our words. Even

The State of Aloneness

pleasant and polite words, if they emerge out of this contaminated mind, produce a jarring sensation in those who hear them. It is not the form of speech that matters so much as the source of speech. Whatever arises from a source that is pure and uncontaminated is bound to be fresh and vital and can cause no wound. An uncontaminated mind is utterly alone; a touch or attachment to anything produces contamination. The mind must be incorruptible before it becomes a source of pure and uncontaminated speech. Thus 'before the voice can speak in the presence of the Master' the corruptible must put on incorruption — the contaminated mind must be rendered pure and unsullied. And the mind that is pure stands absolutely alone. The voice that emerges out of this aloneness can doubtless have no power to wound.

The last of the opening sentences states:

Before the soul can stand in the presence of the Masters its feet must be washed in the blood of the heart.

When does the heart bleed? Obviously it bleeds when the self of man is being crushed — when the personality is being destroyed. The bleeding of the heart is a process of being torn away from the very roots of one's existence. What greater aloneness can there be than that which arises on being separated from oneself? When the heart bleeds, the body must perish. In spiritual terms the bleeding of the heart must result in the perishing of the psychological entity which we call the 'I'. Paradoxically, we can stand before the presence of the Master or God only when we have ceased to exist! According to Eastern tradition one must not enter the Holy of Holies without washing one's feet. It symbolizes an act of purification. How can a soul stand in the presence of the Master unless he is purified? And what greater purification can there be than that which arises out of the annihilation of the self? The self has gathered dust through the ages and built an entity called the 'I'. The 'I' is an accumulation of the past — it is the point where all past memories are focused. How can we enter the Holy of Holies carrying the dust of the ages clinging to our feet? It is the removal of this dust of past memories which causes the heart to bleed. When we are separated from our own past we stand all alone. The past and the future give us company. We cling fast to these companions. We know not what aloneness is so long as they are

The State of Aloneness

with us. It is the 'present' that constitutes a moment of absolute aloneness. Perception can only be in the present — it can never be in the past or in the future. Thus, it is only when we are separated from our past — and therefore from our future — that we can 'see' the Master or Truth. We can stand in the presence of the Master only in the moment of the present when we are absolutely alone, having removed from our feet the dust of past memories. Being purified through a complete separation from our own psychological past as well as future, we are enabled to stand in the presence of the Master. This indeed is the mysterious event about which *Light on the Path* speaks.

The vision of the Master can come to the spiritual pilgrim only when his eyes, ears and speech have been purified. And this purification is the deep experience of aloneness. To see and have no tears; to hear and take no offence; to speak and cause no harm — this is possible only when the mind receives the challenge of life but does not send out any response from its sphere of memories. When there is only challenge and no response the way is found, for the mind is illumined from above. So long as the mind struggles in the dark to find a way, the way cannot be found, for the mind is lost in the jungle of its own projections. It is only when the mind ceases to project — to cast its own shadow — that the path can be seen. 'His Light dwelleth ever in our midst' — but the mind casting its own shadow prevents us from seeing this light. The mind must cast away its opaqueness and be transparent so that the path may be illumined. The transparency of the mind is a state of aloneness, for it has been stripped of everything that it had. It has nothing to hold on to — neither substance nor shadow. This is indeed the supreme spiritual state in which the mind has been rendered mindless.

How to come to this state of aloneness in which the mysterious event occurs, proving to us that the way has been found? This is the main theme of the book, discussed in the chapters that follow.

3

Surrender to the Unknown

In *Light on the Path* there is a profoundly mystical statement which says:

> You will enter the light, but you will never touch the Flame.

It is obvious that this statement indicates the possibilities as well as the limitations of human effort. It suggests that beyond a particular point man cannot proceed, even though his endeavour may be the hardest and the most sincere. The phrase 'You will *never* touch the Flame' can leave no doubt in the mind of the neophyte, for there is no ambiguity about this statement. For a man who undertakes the arduous journey to spiritual heights it is essential to know clearly what are the possibilities of conscious effort and what are its limitations. Without knowing the limitations of conscious effort, we may expect from it *that* which it can never give, and feel frustrated in the end.

It is interesting to find that every great religion of the world has two aspects of expression — the ethical and the spiritual. The exoteric aspect of religion deals with the ethical problems of man. Its approach to life is essentially moral — and a moral approach is concerned with mere modifications in one's way of living. In other words, it is concerned with the cultivation of new habits. It operates in the realm of continuity. The modifications that it seeks to bring about are obviously through conscious effort. The exoteric religion with its moral approach lays a special emphasis on the possibilities of conscious effort.

But there is an esoteric aspect of religion as well. Its basis is spiritual and not ethical. This is not to say that the spiritual is anti-moral. The spiritual approach is neither a continuation of the ethical approach nor is it contrary to it. It is not concerned with mere modifications, with structural changes, with the cultivation of new habits. The spiritual approach deals with the fundamental transformation of man, with the revolution at the centre. The esoteric religion is not a mere extension of the exoteric — it belongs to a new dimension of existence altogether.

Surrender to the Unknown

Frithjof Schuon in his book, *The Transcendent Unity of Religions*, says:

> The presence of an esoteric nucleus in a civilization that is specifically exoteric in character guarantees to it a normal development and a maximum of stability; this nucleus, however, is not in any sense a part, even an inner part, of the exoterism, but represents, on the contrary, a quasi-independent 'dimension' in relation to the latter.

If the exoteric or ethical aspect of religion lays emphasis on the possibilities of conscious effort, the esoteric or spiritual aspect draws our attention to the limitations of conscious effort. To know the limitations of conscious effort is not to cease making efforts with the conscious mind. It only indicates the legitimate sphere of conscious effort. Within this sphere the possibilities of conscious effort must be thoroughly explored. One must not, however, expect to 'touch the flame' as a result of conscious effort. To put it differently, the ethical progress which is the product of conscious effort indicates a movement within one's own dimensional realm. But spiritual transformation brings an intimation of that which transcends one's own dimensional realm. One deals with the extension of consciousness, the other deals with the expansion of consciousness.

There is no doubt that *Light on the Path* deals with spiritual transformation or the expansion of consciousness. This is indicated by the three following aphorisms which precede the statement about entering the light, but not touching the flame. These three aphorisms are:

Desire only that which is within you.
Desire only that which is beyond you.
Desire only that which is unattainable.

The first of these aphorisms seems meaningless on a mere superficial examination of it, for it would amount to desiring that which we already possess! Such a desire would mean a mere accumulation of what we have. In terms of this meaning, 'to desire that which is within' us must result in psychological greed or hoarding. Surely *Light on the Path* does not suggest that the spiritual pilgrim should indulge in psychological greed. This instruction has to be understood in the light of the second aphorism which says:

Desire only that which is beyond you.

Here the neophyte is asked to desire that

Surrender to the Unknown

which he does not possess. Our dreams, fancies and imaginings are indeed beyond us. They are no doubt within us, but still out of our grasp. Are we then asked to follow these dreams and fancies? Are not our dreams and ideals the creations and projections of the mind? If we are to desire the projections of our mind surely we would be caught up in a circle of continuity. The mind moves in a circle. Its movement results in a modified continuity. Usually what we mean by progress is only a modification in structure. To strive for that which is beyond us is indeed a matter of conscious effort. All moral and ethical movements are strivings in the direction of that which is beyond. But a conscious effort cannot result in fundamental spiritual transformation; it can produce only a changed structure, a new pattern of behaviour, for its striving is in the direction of that which the mind has projected. What the mind describes as future is only a modification of the past. The 'beyond' which the mind perceives is only a modification of the 'here'. That which exists outside the sphere of the continuity of thought can never be imagined or dreamt of by the mind.

What then is the meaning of this instruction

about desiring that which is beyond us? To strive for that which is beyond is indeed to explore the possibilities of conscious effort. But if the conscious effort were adequate to effect a spiritual transformation, the third instruction in this particular group of aphorisms would become utterly superfluous. The third instruction says:

Desire only that which is unattainable.

What is the difference between the 'beyond' and the 'unattainable'? The former indicates the possibilities of conscious effort while the latter suggests its limitations. If the beyond and the unattainable were the same there would be no need for two separate aphorisms. But they are not the same. The beyond is something which lies in the future, and therefore can be attained in the course of time. That which separates the 'here' from the 'beyond' is time. But the unattainable has nothing to do with the passage of time. That which can be attained through the process of time is not unattainable. *Light on the Path* says that the flame will *never* be touched. Thus it is not a question of time so far as the touching of the flame is concerned.

Here no consolation of time is given to the

Surrender to the Unknown

neophyte. The unattainable is that which is not within the sphere of attainment. Now to attain is to achieve, accomplish, or reach by effort. To desire the unattainable, therefore, implies desiring that which cannot be reached by conscious effort. It suggests knowing the limitations of conscious effort and being sensitive to that which transcends it. The mind does not know what transcends its frontiers but it can open itself out to receive this transcendental Reality. The unattainable is transcendental. To desire that which is unattainable is to be sensitive to that which is outside the realm of conscious effort. How is the mind to develop this sensitivity?

The mind can develop this sensitivity only by examining its spheres of conscious effort. If the mind can be aware of its operations within this sphere it will soon begin to comprehend the limitations of conscious effort. We have first to know what our spheres of conscious effort are before we can realize the limitations involved in this process.

What are the spheres of man's conscious effort? These are indicated in the three rules which follow the above aphorisms. They are:

Kill out ambition.
Kill out desire of life.
Kill out desire of comfort.

Kill out ambition: What is ambition, whether on the material or on the non-material plane? It is obviously a craving for success — a desire to be *somebody*. Man is afraid of being nobody, of being just what he is. He wants to attract the attention of others, he wants to be recognized. Through ambition, therefore, man seeks significance. He feels that only a successful person will get recognition from others and so in following certain ambitions, material or spiritual, he is striving for success. What does killing out ambition mean? Does it mean working for failure instead of success? Does it mean giving up success? To consciously work towards failure is another way of working for success! It is to succeed by failure! When one strives for failure it is failure that becomes the ambition. Therefore, the killing out of ambition does not suggest giving up success or courting failure.

To kill out ambition is to inquire why we have a craving for success. If success is the sphere of conscious effort, what is it that we hope to achieve by it? It is in this enquiry — and there alone — that the motives for success — or its opposite, failure — will be revealed to our sight. The motives will indicate to us the limitations of our conscious effort. For success has no end. When a man has reached one point of success he realizes that he must move still further. The striving for success or the process of becoming stops nowhere, for in this process 'man never is, but always to be blest'. Man feels that success is ever denied to him. On the path of success, the enquiring man, sooner or later, realizes the limitations of conscious effort. When this happens there is the killing out of ambition.

If man cannot have success he must at least have the joy of continuity. The second aphorism, however, says:

Kill out desire of life.

What does desire of life mean? It is nothing but a craving for continuity. We wish to continue through the things that we have or through the persons with whom we are related or through the ideals and ideas that we cherish. Man is afraid of the moment of discontinuity for it is a moment of absolute aloneness. Like the striving for success, the maintenance of continuity also belongs to the realm of conscious effort. The desire to live is obviously born out of the craving for continuity. Man makes frantic efforts to maintain continuity; but it is not possible for man to maintain a continuity of existence. He can never avoid death even though his efforts in that direction may be of the most strenuous nature. And death is indeed a moment of discontinuity. Thus, both in the achievement of success and in the maintenance of continuity, man's conscious effort has to meet with a 'ring-pass-not', beyond which it cannot proceed.

But man feels that, even though there may be moments of discontinuity and even though success may be denied to him, he can at least have security during the period of continuity and across the gulf of discontinuity. It is to this factor of security that our attention is drawn in the following aphorism:

Kill out desire of comfort.

To desire comfort is to crave security — physical, emotional, mental and spiritual. We want to be assured of security wherever we may be. We want somebody to hold our hand during the darkness of discontinuity. We are afraid to

Surrender to the Unknown

let ourselves go — to surrender ourselves to that darkness.

Thus success, continuity and security represent man's field of conscious effort. In other words, his conscious effort is focused either towards achieving success or maintaining continuity or establishing zones of security. *Light on the Path* re-emphasizes these factors of success, continuity and security in the three further aphorisms, where these factors are presented to us in a subtler form — in a form that is, as it were, spirally higher. This is obviously to show to the neophyte that success, continuity and security lead to frustration at all levels, that there are limitations beyond which conscious effort cannot go. The higher spiral of success, continuity and security is indicated in the three following sentences:

Kill out all sense of separateness.
Kill out desire for sensation.
Kill out the hunger for growth.

Man clings to a sense of separateness because he feels he can be secure only as a separate entity. The mind wants us to believe that if we could establish ourselves in a fixed position we would be utterly secure from the impacts of life.

The flow of life would not disturb us in this isolated spot. But such an existence is impossible, for to be in a position where the flow of life cannot touch us, is verily to stagnate. All sense of separation, therefore, implies stagnation. Thus security through a sense of separation is possible only in a condition of non-existence! All such efforts at seeking security are, therefore, utterly meaningless, for they are destined to fail. To realize for oneself that isolation can never lead us to security is indeed to kill out all sense of separateness.

We are further asked to kill out desire for sensation. Are we then to be dull and dead to the impacts of life? What after all is desire for sensation? It is a subtle form of craving for continuity. Continuity is the maintenance of an unbroken chain of relationship between the environmental challenge and the psychological response. To be in a state of challenge without any reaction of the mind is to be in a condition of storm and disturbance. We avoid storms and disturbances by pursuing and maintaining an unbroken chain of reactions. Thus 'desire for sensation' is an effort of the mind to avoid moments of discontinuity or loneliness.

Surrender to the Unknown

Sometimes the challenges of life are so overwhelming that the chain of reactions, zealously guarded by the mind, snaps, causing a break in continuity. No amount of effort by the mind can avoid the arrival of this moment of discontinuity.

This book of Mysticism asks the spiritual pilgrim to kill even the hunger for growth. If hunger for growth is to be killed what incentive is left for the neophyte to move on? Has the spiritual journey to be conducted without any incentive? Does hunger for growth help the candidate on his spiritual journey? It must be remembered that hunger for growth is only a subtle form of ambition or desire for success. Man wants to reach greater and greater spiritual heights. But why does he want to ascend higher and higher? If there is a hunger to rise higher and higher, it is probably because man wants to feel that he is superior to others. He wants to become significant by this feeling of superiority. If he can show to others that he has succeeded where many have failed, then he would assume a significant position. Thus behind the hunger for growth there is a desire for success. If ambition is the lower rung of the ladder of success, hunger for growth is the higher. Both form part of the same process.

Is spiritual attainment possible in the satisfying of the hunger for growth? By conscious effort no growth or expansion is possible — all that is possible is only an extension of consciousness. Spiritual transformation, however, represents a higher dimension of existence. It is an expansion of consciousness. Since it belongs to a higher dimension it is outside the purview of conscious effort. How can mind by its efforts reach something which transcends its sphere of operations? Mind can achieve only that which is within its own sphere of continuity. A higher dimension is not within the continuity of the lower dimension. It is unattainable in terms of the mind and its conscious efforts. When man realizes this, the hunger for growth disappears — for he knows that what he was hungering for was not growth but only a continuity through success.

The possibilities and the limitations of conscious effort, which we have discussed in this chapter, contain the great mystical truth of the ascent and descent in spiritual life. We can doubtless ascend upto a particular point by conscious effort, but after that there must come a descent into us of a power that is outside the

Surrender to the Unknown 47

sphere of attainment by the mind. This descent will happen, provided we are open and sensitive, having divested all craving for success, continuity and security.

Light on the Path says:

> Grow as the flower grows, unconsciously, but eagerly anxious to open its soul to the air. So must you press forward to open your soul to the Eternal. But it must be the Eternal that draws forth your strength and beauty, not desire for growth. For, in the one case you develop in the luxuriance of purity; in the other you harden by the forcible passion for personal stature.

The Eternal drawing forth strength and beauty is indeed the phenomenon of descent. A mere conscious effort creates a hardening of one's nature. Where both the possibility and limitation of conscious effort are understood, there we have spiritual transformation in the luxuriance of purity. In the luxuriance of purity there takes place the miracle play of Ascent and Descent.

By conscious effort one can only enter the Light; it is only in the moment of supreme unconsciousness, the moment of absolute aloneness, when we are not even with ourselves, that the great miracle of touching the flame occurs. It is the hour of descent when the sea enters the dewdrop.

How is one to be prepared for this great hour of descent?

4

The Discovery of the Path

There are three rules in *Light on the Path* which on first reading seem utterly meaningless against the background of what has been discussed so far. Having indicated to the neophyte that he must kill out ambition, desire of life and desire of comfort, the book asks him to:

Desire power ardently.
Desire peace fervently.
Desire possessions above all.

These rules seem absolutely contrary to the instructions given in the earlier part of the book. By themselves they seem to point to the path of black magic. On superficial examination and taking the rules in isolation, it looks as if the neophyte is required to move along the path of rank materialism. To desire power ardently and to desire possessions above all — is this not the path that the man of the world takes in order to achieve material success? These rules seem to be bringing back success, continuity and security after they have been rejected in the earlier part of the book. For power goes with success, as peace and possessions go with continuity and security respectively. What should the neophyte do? Should he reject the path of success, continuity and security, or should he tread along the direction indicated by them? The spiritual pilgrim is indeed thrown into a welter of confusion by these seemingly contradictory instructions.

No doubt these three rules make no sense when taken in isolation. The question is, why have they been given? In order to understand their meaning we have to examine them against the background of the aphorism just preceding them. The three rules immediately follow the instruction in which the neophyte is asked to 'desire that which is unattainable'. We have seen in the last chapter that the 'unattainable' is that which cannot be reached by conscious effort. The 'unattainable' is not to be confused with the 'beyond'. In being open and sensitive to that which is 'unattainable', the mind comes to a condition in which it sees nothing but a deep chasm or wide gulf before it. It faces unending darkness. There is nothing to mitigate

The Discovery of the Path

the severity of that darkness, for there is no 'beyond' from where a ray of light may come to illumine the path of the mind. The mind is utterly lonely with nothing to hold on to — the past, that is, the psychological past having vanished with the realization of the limitations of conscious effort, and the future nowhere to be perceived. It finds no bridge across the chasm to help it enter the unknown, nor can it return, for the past, composed of success, continuity and security, has dropped away in the realization of their falseness. What is the mind to do in front of this fearful, dark chasm?

It is the condition of the mind standing at this precipice which has been described in the three rules above. The condition to which the mind has come is of tremendous acuteness. This acuteness is indicated by the use of such words as 'ardently', 'fervently' and 'above all'. The mind is in a state of great intensity or tension. It is extraordinarily alert; it is acutely wakeful; it is undistracted. For, how can the mind be distracted on the brink of a precipice? It is the past and the future that distract the mind. But both these have disappeared, and therefore there is nothing but ardent wakefulness on the part of the mind. It cannot go to sleep on the brink of a precipice lest it fall into the deep abyss; nor can it move, for there is nowhere to go. It is alert and yet not moving; and it is this which creates the state of tremendous acuteness. This acuteness or ardent wakefulness is not merely at the thinking level. It covers all the faculties of man. In other words, the man in his entire being has come to this extraordinary wakefulness. No effort through any of the faculties that he possesses helps him to find the way. Thus the acuteness of the entire being of man has been depicted in those three rules quoted above.

'To desire power ardently' describes the ideational acuteness of man. Power is associated with ideas — the thought-operations of the mind. The power of thought has been recognized in all the psychological and philosophical literatures of the world. Whatever the power man wields over his environment, it is through his faculty of thought. On the brink of a spiritual precipice it is therefore natural for the mind to desire power ardently. It seeks some power by which the darkness can be chased away. It has realized that its own powers are of no avail. It is ardently seeking for some power that may be vouchsafed

The Discovery of the Path

to it. It is this tension of the mind that has been expressed in this phrase: Desire power ardently.

If power represents the thinking faculty, peace refers to human relationship. Facing darkness where no way is found, man naturally experiences a tension at the emotional level too. Peace is a condition of emotional balance. The spiritual pilgrim 'desires peace fervently' in this hour of great trial. This indeed is emotional sensitivity. Thus in this instruction the neophyte is asked to maintain extraordinary responsiveness at the emotional level.

Then we come to the third instruction in this particular group of aphorisms which says: Desire possessions above all. Possessions deal with things, even as power and peace refer to ideas and persons respectively. This instruction, therefore, has a bearing on the state of physical senses. When a person desires possessions above all, his senses are alert and discriminating lest he lose possessions or acquire possessions of an inferior quality. All the senses need to be very sensitive, and that is what happens when one is on the edge of a precipice.

Thus the three instructions describe the condition of man's entire being when he faces an acute situation. His mind, emotions and senses have to be alert, in order to 'catch the faintest whisper' in the midst of surrounding darkness. A man divested of a desire for success, continuity and security finds that there is no ground on which he can stand. He is seeking some foothold in the midst of this acute situation. It is this search for a foothold which is characterized by extraordinary sensitivity of mind, emotions and the physical senses. These three are in a condition of sleepless vigilance. In no part of his being can the spiritual pilgrim afford to be asleep. He has to keep a constant vigil throughout the night. Not a wink of sleep is possible on the brink of the precipice where he stands. In front of the unattainable, which is the unknown, man must be wide awake in all parts of his nature.

This extraordinary sensitivity is possible for the spiritual pilgrim because all his distractions in the form of success, continuity and security have vanished. A distracted mind can never be sensitive, for it is bound to dart off into various directions. This sensitivity is the result of man's realization of the limitations of his conscious effort. As long as man functions within the realms of the possibilities of conscious effort, so long is

The Discovery of the Path

he not face to face with an acute situation. In the realm of conscious effort, man is bound to be distracted because of the various alternatives that he sees. It is only when all the alternatives to a situation are put away that the problem becomes acute. And the dissolution of a problem occurs only when the mind is not in a position to dart off into alternative paths. It is by examining the spheres of one's conscious efforts, by examining one's efforts along success, continuity and security, that one can arrive at the acuteness of a problem. In this acuteness the mind is very sensitive, ready to receive whatever descends from the realms unknown to it.

The question is: How can one's problems be dissolved in this acuteness of the mind? What happens when the mind is in this state? Here we are helped by the three rules that follow the instruction regarding desire for power, peace and possessions. These are:

Seek out the way.
Seek the way by retreating within.
Seek the way by advancing boldly without.

As long as the mind is caught up in the movement of choosing alternatives, so long it cannot find the way. In choosing alternatives the mind is following its own projections. Such a mind is bound to go astray. The following passage from the writings of Asvaghosha, the great Buddhist philosopher, makes this particular point clear. He says:

> A man who is lost, goes astray because he is bent on pursuing a certain direction; and his confusion has no valid foundation other than that he is bent on a certain direction.

Only that mind in acute sensitivity, standing on a precipice, is in a position to observe even the slightest hint that may come from realms unknown to it. Being in a state of aloneness it can hear even the faintest whisper that may come from the unattainable. Since the mind is not occupied by its own interests, it is perfectly open and responsive. The instruction 'Seek out the way' is obviously addressed to such a mind and not to a mind bent upon following a particular direction.

But what will be the field of observation for such a mind? This is indicated in the two rules that follow which speak about 'retreating within' and 'advancing boldly without'.

The Discovery of the Path

The neophyte is asked to seek the way by retreating within. But what is there to see within when desires for success, continuity and security have dropped away and the limitations of conscious effort are realized? If the mind has become divested of all its content, what is there to see within? Even when the mind is emptied of all its contents, there still lurks the desire to name this emptiness. The naming of an experience is the last frantic effort of the mind to hold on to something. Round about the name it can restart all its activities towards security, continuity and success. In order to name anything the mind has to establish a centre of recognition. At this centre of recognition the mind tries to settle down so that it can escape from the loneliness that otherwise faces it. The naming of an experience is like catching at a straw by the mind while it is afraid of being drowned under the enveloping darkness. The neophyte is, therefore, asked to retreat within in order to observe whether the mind is engaged in this subtle process of naming the experience of emptiness. If it does then the way cannot be found, for the mind will follow only the direction indicated by its projections. Needless to say that in the very awareness of this process of naming in which the mind is engaged, the process ceases. And it is this which is suggested by the phrase: 'Seek the way by retreating within.' It is in this seeking that the mind is freed from even the subtlest of its projections.

When the mind has moved away from the process of naming an experience, from the act of naming even the experience of emptiness, it is then that the neophyte can 'seek the way by boldly advancing without'. When can one advance boldly? Only when there is nothing to hold one back. When there are no projections of the mind, not even the subtlest, holding back the neophyte, then, and then only, can he boldly advance.

To seek the way by boldly advancing without is to have an absolutely objective view of life. It means seeing things as they are. We are not able to advance boldly because the mind's projections hold us back. And these projections prevent us from seeing things in their proper perspective. In order to advance boldly without, one must have a 'right perception of things objective'. Without this right perspective our bold advance may result in grievous injury to ourselves. Only with an objective view of life can one hear the faintest whisper. The way can be found only when the voices of the mind have been silenced. As the neophyte retreats within to observe the mind's subtlest endeavours to seek security, which is by naming an experience, this condition of silence comes into existence. And when silence reigns within, the neophyte is enabled to see things as they are. With the withering away of all centres of psychological recognition, the mind is completely free, and it is only a free mind that can boldly advance. No matter what the incidents and events of life may be, such a mind is able to see the way. It shrinks from no experience because it cannot be caught anywhere or by anything. It is the mind tethered to a fixed point, the mind with centres of psychological vested interest, that is afraid to move. A free mind feels no bondage and no compulsion of karma. It is perfectly objective in its approach to life, neither identifying with, nor repulsed by, any situation.

Light on the Path says:

> . . . remember that the soiled garment you shrink from touching, may have been yours yesterday, may be yours tomorrow. And if you turn with horror from it when it is flung upon your shoulders, it will cling the more closely to you. The self-righteous man makes for himself a bed of mire.

To advance boldly without requires the mind's freedom from all vested interest. The self-righteous man never advances boldly without, for he has his vested interest in the virtue to which he clings lest he may be dispossessed of it. He who is conscious of his virtue is tethered by that virtue. It becomes a centre of resistance so that he shrinks from all such experiences that threaten to dispossess him of that which he zealously guards. To advance boldly without, is to have a mind that is free from the process both of justification and condemnation. To such a person karma has no terror, for he is able to see his way clearly no matter how thick the forest of events and happenings that constitute his daily life.

The mind that is free and not tethered to any idea is unafraid of the precipice on which it stands. The darkness is no darkness at all to a mind that is free from the process of even naming an experience. The darkness appears fearsome to a mind that has named it. Having named it, the mind shrinks from it, condemning it as something dangerous and unholy. But when the process of naming has ceased, the mind is able to perceive *what is* in perfect objectivity. To advance boldly without is indeed a surrender to *what is* — a

The Discovery of the Path

surrender that is utterly unconscious. When we can see things and events as they are, then the things and events convey their secrets to us. It is in the silence of aloneness, when there is no movement of thought, that the mysterious event will occur which will 'prove that the way has been found'. This is the thrilling moment of discovery, the sacred hour when the flower blooms.

It is through the unconscious surrender of the mind to the unknown and the unattainable that the thrilling experience of discovery comes. In this moment of surrender man knows that he has 'found the beginning of the Way'. Having been shaken up by the storm, having faced aloneness and having surrendered oneself to the unattainable, there comes the great moment of discovery. *Light on the Path* describes this moment thus:

> Call it by what name you will, it is a voice that speaks where there is none to speak — it is a messenger that comes, a messenger without form or substance; or it is the flower of the soul that has opened.

The discovery of the path is indeed the opening of the flower of the soul. It is in the unconscious surrender to the unattainable, in the hour of absolute aloneness, that this mysterious event occurs.

The Path has been discovered and now we must commence the treading of that Path.

5

The Fighter and the Warrior

The first part of *Light on the Path* leads us to the discovery of the path through storm, aloneness and surrender. In the second part, the book is concerned with the treading of the Path. It is obvious that one cannot tread the path before one has discovered it — and yet it is this obvious truth which is forgotten by most of the people making frantic efforts to walk on the spiritual path. It is when we try to tread the path before discovering it that problems of discipline and struggle arise. An intellectual understanding, which in the ultimate analysis is only familiarity with words, is not what can be called discovery. One may collect all the information about the path from books or from hearsay, but such a collection of information can, by no stretch of imagination, be called a discovery. Most men prepare themselves to tread the path on the basis of the information that has been collected. No wonder that such treading results in tiredness, exhaustion and frustration! The element of joy vanishes when the treading is attempted before discovery. To tread the path before discovery is only to imitate a particular pattern of conduct as indicated in books. It is an effort to mould and shape one's life in terms of that pattern. This is exactly what ordinarily is understood as discipline. But a process of imitation is devoid of all creative joy. And without creativity, a journey on the spiritual path is meaningless. Thus, discovery before the candidate begins his journey is of fundamental importance, for it is only in the background of discovery that one can feel the creative joy of life. To discover the path is to determine the right starting point. In discovery one comes to the 'beginning of the way'. Giordano Bruno, the great Italian philosopher, uttered a profound truth when he said: 'If the first button of your coat is wrongly buttoned, all the rest are crooked.' To discover the path is to see that the first button of our coat is rightly buttoned. Having discovered the right starting point the treading of the path becomes natural and spontaneous, without an element of forcing oneself to become what one is not. The treading of the path appears full of hard

The Fighter and the Warrior

discipline only when the right starting point has not been found.

In the *Bhagavadgitā* there is a statement:

> However men approach Me, even so do I welcome them, for the paths men take from every side are Mine.

This statement suggests that there are innumerable paths to Reality and so what does it matter where we start? On a superficial examination of this sentence it appears that the discovery of a right starting point is after all not very essential. As against this there is a statement in one of the Upanishad-s: 'There is no other Path at all to go', obviously meaning thereby that there is only one Path to Reality. How can these two statements be reconciled? Are there many paths to Reality or is there only one? Strangely enough both these statements are absolutely correct. There is no doubt that there are as many paths as there are individuals but each individual can take only that path which he has discovered for himself. Thus there is no other path to go save the one that is discovered by the individual. But since discovery has to be individual and not collective, there will be as many discoveries as there are individuals. And so the starting point of the spiritual journey will differ from individual to individual, and yet each starting point will have its source of emanation only in that which the individual has discovered. There is indeed no other path to go except the path discovered by each man for himself.

But what after all does discovery mean? In the first place, discovery can come about only with reference to that which exists. In other words, existence must precede discovery. It is quite obvious that we cannot discover that which does not exist. The mind may invent something that did not exist before — but then an invention of the mind and discovery are two different things. An invention is the product of the mind while discovery is the perception of what already exists. There is another factor essential for the understanding of what is known as discovery. And that is, discovery implies seeing something for the first time. By bringing these two concepts together one may say that discovery indicates seeing for the first time something that already exists. There may be quite a large number of things round about us which might not have been discovered by us because we have not seen them.

The Fighter and the Warrior 67

Needless to say that we can discover a thing only when we see it. Unless there is an awareness in one's consciousness about a thing which exists there cannot be any discovery with reference to that thing. In short, observation is fundamental to discovery.

Now, the discovery of a physical thing differs from discovering a psychological phenomenon. We are discussing here the problem of discovering the spiritual path. The spiritual path has no physical location — it is a psychological phenomenon. A physical object is comparatively static but a psychological phenomenon is intensely dynamic. It is in a fluidic state. It is so dynamic that if you want to see it where it was, you cannot! It has moved away. Our psychological setting is new every moment — not so much as to its pattern but as to its content. Since the spiritual path is not apart from our daily existence and since the psychological setting of that existence constantly changes, the path has to be discovered again and again, from moment to moment. To discover is really to un-cover. The path gets covered up in the new setting and that is why its discovery is a constant process. But would not the process of constant discovery prove tiresome and monotonous? Monotony and discovery do not go together. Discovery has a thrill about it. Even though the path has to be discovered from moment to moment, every moment of such discovery is full of a thrilling experience. The neophyte will have the thrill of seeing the path for the first time whenever he discovers it in the new psychological setting.

The spiritual path plays hide-and-seek with the neophyte. In Hindu mythology there is an episode of Lord Śri Kṛshna playing hide-and-seek with the Gopi-s — the cowherd maidens. The Gopi-s felt as if they were seeing Śri Kṛshna for the first time whenever they discovered him in this game of hide-and-seek. Such was the thrilling experience of the Gopi-s that the process of discovering Śri Kṛshna never seemed dull or monotonous to them. This episode depicts the great mystic truth of the joy of discovering the path constantly in the midst of ever-changing psychological settings.

It is this element of constant discovery of the path which differentiates spirituality from morality. Morality is a movement in terms of an established code. It is an adjustment to the structure or pattern of life. Spirituality, on the other hand, is concerned with discovering the content or the spirit ensouling a structure, and as such implies a life that is lived from moment to moment. Spirituality does not deal with the generalizations of life — it deals with the individualities of life. But then in spiritual life are we not concerned with such problems as anger, greed, envy, etc.? And is not anger a generalization of a particular psychological state? It is true that there is a factor of generalization in the state known as anger. But then such a generalization is only at the verbal level. Even though we use the word 'anger' to denote a particular state, the content of anger differs from individual to individual. Not only that, each incident of anger has an individuality of its own. Between the various incidents of anger the common factor is only the word. But the word anger is not anger at all — it is the content of an incident or event which is anger. And the content of anger does not lend itself to generalization.

Since each psychological moment has an individuality of its own and since our psychological setting is an ever-changing phenomenon, the spiritual path has to be discovered from moment to moment. In the midst of our day-to-day existence we have constantly to find the way.

And the secret of finding the way has been described in the first part of *Light on the Path*. It is in man's surrender to the unknown and the unattainable that the mysterious event occurs which 'proves that the way has been found'. Such surrender comes only in the moment of absolute aloneness caused by the raging of psychological storms tearing the man away from the very roots of his existence. The discovery of the path occurs only in moments of complete surrender.

The discovery of the path constitutes only the starting point of the journey. The whole path still lies untrodden. We need to remember that in the background of discovery, the treading of the path becomes a matter of intense joy. The mind having been filled with the thrill of discovery, is able to give its full and undistracted attention to every detail connected with the treading of the path. There is a new strength which the neophyte feels within his heart because of this discovery. *Light on the Path* says:

> The silence may last a moment of time, or it may last a thousand years. But it will end. Yet you will carry its strength with you.

The discovery occurs in the self-surrender

which follows absolute aloneness or silence. This moment of silence may be short or long — the duration of time does not matter — yet it will reveal to the man a vision that will fill his entire being. The moment of silence is indeed the moment of man's renewal. The new strength that he has gained out of the vision will enable him to tread the path with a song in his heart.

One may say that the discovery of the Path is a journey *to* God, the Master or Truth, while the treading of the Path is a journey *with* God, the Master or Truth. He who has discovered the path journeys on that path in company with the Master himself. The Master walks with him — and can the treading of the path be ever tiresome under these circumstances? The discovery of the path is indeed the discovery of the Master, Truth or God. From that moment of discovery every detail of our daily existence, where alone the treading of the path must occur, assumes a new significance. But the journey with the Master is not possible without the discovery of the Master. *Light on the Path* says:

... when the disciple is ready, the Master is ready also.

The readiness of the disciple consists in his

complete self-surrender which truly is the state in which he discovers the Master. Thus, from that moment onwards the Master walks with the disciple. The Path is no longer the Path of Woe — it is the Path of indescribable Joy. This journey with the Master has been described in the following three aphorisms with which the second part of *Light on the Path* begins:

1. *Stand aside in the coming battle, and though thou fightest, be not thou the Warrior.*
2. *Look for the Warrior and let him fight in thee.*
3. *Take his orders for battle and obey them.*

Here we are reminded of the instruction that Śri Kṛshna gave to Arjuna on the field of battle. He was asked to be an instrument, a channel. In other words, he was required to be a fighter, not a warrior. *Light on the Path* makes a distinction between a fighter and a warrior. A fighter is, in this context, an agent, a channel of the warrior. The warrior is the transcendental Reality or Truth while the fighter represents the mind of man. In the treading of the path if we could let truth solve the problems of life we would never fail. Instead, with the capacities of the mind we try to solve the

The Fighter and the Warrior

problem and miserably fail in the attempt. The mind can formulate a problem; it cannot solve it. Once again we are dealing with the possibilities and the limitations of conscious effort. *Light on the Path* says:

> Look for the Warrior and let him fight in thee.

In other words, discover the warrior and act as his instrument in carrying out his orders. If we do not look for the warrior but fight the battle on the strength of our own limited perception, we are sure to lose the battle. We fail again and again in the battles of life because instead of acting as fighters we arrogate to ourselves the role of the warrior!

The looking for the warrior has to go on all the time. If we lose sight of him even for a moment, confusion and chaos will arise in the battles of life. But the question is: If we 'stand aside in the coming battle' and 'look for the warrior', are we not likely to be passive in our entire approach to life? Shall we not develop a tendency of looking up to him in every moment of difficulty? Does *Light on the Path* indicate to us a passive approach to life? Here we must understand clearly the twofold instruction that is given. It says:

1. Look for the Warrior and let him fight in thee.
2. Take his orders for battle and obey them.

Looking for the warrior is a negative approach. We can look for the warrior — we can discover him — only in self-surrender born out of absolute aloneness. It is in absolute negativity that the warrior can be discovered. As long as the mind visualizes possibilities of conscious effort, with reference to a problem, the warrior must remain undiscovered. Only when the struggles of the mind in the direction of success, continuity and security have ceased, can the warrior be discovered.

But *Light on the Path* does not merely say: 'Look for the Warrior.' It also says: 'Let him fight in thee.' What is meant by letting him fight in us? This is explained in the third aphorism which asks the neophyte to take the orders of the warrior for the battle and obey them. This is indeed a positive approach — though the positive is in the background of the negative. In treading the path the neophyte is asked to carry out the orders of the warrior — and not his own orders. It is to be remembered that complications arise in the battles of our life because it is we who begin

The Fighter and the Warrior

to give orders. The mind not realizing its limitations issues orders for the battle. In fact such is the cleverness of the mind that one of its parts issues the order and the other part tries to carry it out. The part that issues the order is commonly described as the higher mind, and the part that is expected to carry out the order is usually known as the lower mind. By splitting itself into two the mind arrogates to itself the role of a warrior. But the warrior is not the higher mind — he transcends all realms of the mind. *Light on the Path* says:

> ... he is thyself, yet infinitely wiser and stronger than thyself.

To look for the warrior and let him fight in us, by taking his orders and obeying them, is indeed to show forth positivity in the background of negativity. It is 'action in inaction', to use the phrase of the *Bhagavadgitā* — and this truly is the secret of the treading of the path. In our daily life we have to act; in fact, not even for one moment can man exist without action. But the action will be right only when we are not the actor — but only an instrument, a channel. When God, Truth or the Master is the actor and mind the instrument, then there is produced an exquisitely beautiful song of life. It is when we cease to play our tune but only provide an instrument that the Master musician can manifest himself as divine harmony through us. To provide a well-tuned instrument — this indeed is the secret of our daily task.

Now, a well-tuned instrument is tense — its strings being taut — for it has passed through the storms of tuning and has come to absolute aloneness. A tuned instrument is alone for it stands by itself. It is only when the instrument surrenders itself completely in its moment of tenseness to the musician that the divine music becomes possible. When the instrument is ready the singer too is ready. When the warrior fights in us — then the battle can never be lost. *Light on the Path* says:

> When once he has entered thee and become thy Warrior, he will never utterly desert thee.

Thus it is that, after discovery, the neophyte treads the path in the company of the Master. When an action is performed in the background of inaction then it is the Master acting through the disciple. This indeed is the meaning of the aphorism: 'Though thou fightest, be not thou the Warrior.' And with the Master by our side we can

The Fighter and the Warrior

never strike even one blow amiss. *Light on the Path* has beautifully summed up this whole problem of the Fighter and the Warrior in the following passage:

> Look for him, else in the fever and hurry of the fight thou mayest pass him; and he will not know thee unless thou knowest him. If thy cry reach his listening ear then will he fight in thee and fill the dull void within. And if this is so, then canst thou go through the fight cool and unwearied, standing aside and letting him battle for thee. Then it will be impossible for thee to strike one blow amiss. But if thou look not for him, if thou pass him by, then there is no safeguard for thee. Thy brain will reel, thy heart grow uncertain, and in the dust of the battlefield thy sight and senses will fail and thou wilt not know thy friends from thy enemies.

The void created by aloneness will be filled by the Master in the moment of discovery. When the Master is the Warrior fighting through the disciple the battle is won, for no blow can be struck amiss. The disciple can go through life in a cool and unwearied manner because of the Master being all the time by his side. But if the disciple, instead of playing the role of a fighter arrogates to himself the role of the Warrior too, then will his 'brain reel' and his heart 'grow uncertain'. This was what happened to Arjuna when 'in the dust of the battlefield' his 'sight and senses' failed him, when he threw away the arms refusing to fight. Arjuna was the bravest of the brave and yet his heart became uncertain and his brain started reeling. He addressed Lord Śri Kṛshna on the battlefield thus:

> My heart is weighed down with the vice of faintness; my mind is confused as to duty.

Why did this happen to Arjuna on the field of battle? Because he forgot his role. He thought he was the Warrior, while, in fact, he was required only to be a Fighter. The whole theme of the *Bhagavadgitā* centres round this concept of the Fighter and the Warrior, of action in inaction. In the field of Kurukshetra, Śri Kṛshna did not fight, He was the Warrior — the Great Charioteer. It was Arjuna who was the Fighter, but the battle was won only when he fought as an instrument, a channel, of the Warrior. When he saw the confusion of his mind, when he realized that he was arrogating to himself the role of the Warrior, then he declared: 'I will do according to Thy word.' When Arjuna recognized the Warrior and let him fight in him — when he took his orders for

The Fighter and the Warrior

battle from the Warrior and obeyed them — then was the great battle won. Arjuna represents the prowess of man, the possibilities of conscious effort, the element of action, while Śri Kṛshna represents inaction and symbolizes the Transcendental Spirit which is unattainable and, therefore, outside the reach of man's conscious effort. When there is a coexistence of action and inaction, the positive and the negative, then is the treading of the Path a journey with the Master. Rightly does the *Bhagavadgitā* say:

> Wherever is Kṛshna, the Lord of Yoga, wherever is Partha, the archer, assured are there prosperity, victory and happiness.

If in treading the Path through the incidents and the events of daily existence man could perform the miracle of action in inaction, the miracle of a coexistence of the Warrior and the Fighter, then would victory in life's battle be assured to him, for no blow would be struck amiss.

But is it possible for man to perform this miracle in the midst of his mundane existence?

6

The Creative Silence

The secret of treading the Path has been indicated to the neophyte in the very first aphorism with which the second part of *Light on the Path* begins. In terms of this instruction the spiritual pilgrim must become an instrument, a focus, for the expression of the Transcendental Spirit. Now, an instrument, if it is to be effective, must have both negative as well as positive qualities. Firstly, it has to be well tuned, and secondly, in this tuned-up condition, it must completely surrender itself to the singer. This, as we have already seen, is action in inaction.

Light on the Path lays great stress on the negative and positive qualities of an effective instrument. They constitute the Discovery of the Path and the Treading of the Path. To look for the Warrior is to discover the path; to take his orders and obey them is to tread the path. In other words, the spiritual pilgrim must clearly distinguish between the Fighter and the Warrior. Now, there are two dangers involved in not clearly understanding the roles of the fighter and the warrior. If we expect the warrior to become the fighter — then we relapse into utter passivity, into non-action. Similarly, when the fighter arrogates to himself the role of the warrior — then there arise confusion and frustration. The ordinary man of religion is subjected to the first danger, for he expects God to fight his battles; without clearly understanding the possibilities of conscious effort, he passively waits for the grace of God to descend. But an idealist falls prey to the second danger, for he is too positive, not realizing the limitations of man's conscious effort. While the ordinary man of religion is not aware of his own strength, the idealist is too sure of his own powers. The one regards negativity to mean utter passivity, while the other confuses positivity with overconfidence.

In the battles of life it is possible for man to draw upon the strength of the warrior. But often in his arrogance he clings fast to his own limited strength and so, being overconfident, loses the game of life again and again. In the great Hindu epic, the *Mahābhārata*, there is an incident which aptly illustrates these two tendencies of over-confidence in one's own strength and complete surrender to the Greater Strength of the Warrior. When the two royal families of the Pāndava-s and the Kaurava-s finally decided to settle their differences by recourse to war, they both naturally sought the help of Śri Krshna. Duryodhana, the chief among the Kaurava-s, and Arjuna, the matchless fighter among the Pāndava-s, approached Śri Krshna so as to solicit his help. They accidently arrived almost at the same time at the palace of Śri Krshna, Duryodhana being ahead of Arjuna by a few seconds. When they reached Śri Krshna's inner apartment, He was resting. They thought it fit not to disturb him, and so waited near his bed. Duryodhana seated himself on a chair near the head of Śri Krshna, while Arjuna, though a close friend of Śri Krshna, stood near his feet with folded hands. When Śri Krshna awoke from his sleep, his eyes first fell on Arjuna as he was near his feet. This made Duryodhana extremely nervous, for he feared that Arjuna would be given the first choice by Śri Krshna. He, therefore, pleaded with Śri Krshna that since he had reached the palace earlier than Arjuna, he was entitled to have the first choice. But Śri Krshna stated that, on waking, as He had seen Arjuna first it was the latter who must have the first choice and besides Arjuna was younger and so he was entitled to have his say first. And so Śrī Kṛshna offered the choice to Arjuna. He said: 'On the one hand there is my army consisting of brave and dauntless soldiers who are matchless in their fighting qualities, and on the other there is myself. Whichever party selects me must, however, know that I shall not fight.' When Arjuna was asked to choose, he unhesitatingly said he wanted Śrī Kṛshna and not his army on his side. Duryodhana was overjoyed at this choice made by Arjuna for he thought Arjuna had made a fool of himself by having Śrī Kṛshna on his side and rejecting the army of such valiant fighters. Duryodhana was, therefore, happy to have the entire army of Śrī Kṛshna on his side. But the story of the *Mahābhārata* says that the Kaurava-s, with Duryodhana as their Chief, were defeated.

This incident contains a profound mystical Truth. Duryodhana fought only with his own strength, overconfident of his prowess. He chose not only to be a fighter, but the warrior too! In selecting Śrī Kṛshna's army he chose the path of quantity. He was sure that with his quantitative strength increased, due to the addition of Śri Kṛshna's army, he would be able to defeat the Pāndava-s. Arjuna, on the other hand, in choosing Śri Kṛshna chose the path of quality. Arjuna was no mean fighter — he was indeed the bravest of the brave. He was fully conscious of the possibilities of his own power. But he wanted to have this power to be used as an instrument of the Greater Wisdom of Śri Kṛshna. He did not want Śri Kṛshna to fight his battle — he wanted him as the Warrior. If Śri Kṛshna could be the Charioteer guiding his war-chariot then that was enough for Arjuna. To surrender his strength as an instrument to be used by Śri Kṛshna — this was sufficient to win victory over the army of the Kaurava-s. Arjuna fought the battle not merely with his own strength but with the strength of his Master. To his power was added the grace of Śri Kṛshna. He had the courage to surrender his own strength to his Master. It was this courage which he displayed when he chose the Master and not his army. He had faith in his Master and so he could lay all that he had at his feet. Realizing the limitations of his own prowess he was filled with the greater strength of his Master. Quantity did not distract him for he had unshakable faith in the quality.

The Creative Silence

This indeed is the difference between the man of the world and the man of spirituality. The man of the world chooses quantity, but the man of spiritual insight chooses quality. This episode in the *Mahābhārata* is a supreme example of positivity in the background of negativity.

The question is: Can we all show forth this spiritual quality of action in the background of inaction? How to steer clear of the two extremes of overconfidence and utter passivity? How to discover the background of inaction in the midst of our daily activities?

Here we are given further help due to the instructions contained in the aphorisms that follow. *Light on the Path* asks the neophyte to 'listen to the Song of Life'.

But where is the song of life? Life for most men is anything but a song. It is a discord, a conflict, a bitter struggle. The Lord Buddha declared twenty-five centuries ago that 'misery is greater than happiness'. In the midst of our daily activities we hear plenty of noise — but very little of song. If our life could be a song there would be immense delight in treading the path. If our actions could be performed in the background of inaction then there would be a possibility of listening to the song of life. *Light on the Path* has indicated that if we can look for the warrior and let him fight in us then we can go 'through the fight cool and unwearied'. To listen to the song of life is indeed to go through the fight in this cool and unwearied manner. But how can one listen to the song of life in the midst of the daily toil and torture?

This idea of the song of life has not been presented to us in jest or to sport with our feelings — it has been presented to the neophyte in all seriousness. We can understand the serious import of this aphorism only as we understand it in the light of the two following aphorisms. The entire group of these three aphorisms is as follows:

> *Listen to the song of Life.*
> *Store in your memory the melody you hear.*
> *Learn from it the lesson of harmony.*

Life can indeed become a song if we can hear the melody and learn from it the lesson of harmony. What does the hearing of a melody mean? Melody and harmony are terms of music. Indian music is characterized by its melody while Western music has harmony as its outstanding feature. Now a melody is a succession of single

The Creative Silence

notes while in harmony there is a succession of simultaneous or combined notes. In the succession of single notes there is a movement from one fixed note to another. Thus there is an interval between two notes. The charm and grace of a melody lies not in starting from, or arriving at, the fixed note but in the interval between these two notes. The originality of the musician, the richness of his imagination, consists in what he does during this interval. The quality of music is to be perceived in this interval. The freedom of the musician lies in this interval, for he is restricted so far as the maintenance of the two fixed notes is concerned. He cannot change the position of these fixed notes. But surely he can give a free play to his imagination in the interval that separates the fixed notes. Thus, to hear the melody is to listen to the interval between the two notes.

And so if we would listen to the song of life, we must first become aware of the interval between two sounds — the interval between two actions. We are not able to listen to the song of life because we hear only the sounds and not the interval between the sounds; we look only to actions and not the interval between actions. To be aware of the interval is indeed to listen to the silence. But we never listen to the silence. We see, hear, touch only that which is expressed — never do we listen to the interval — the silence — between two expressions. If we could listen to the silence of each other instead of listening merely to the spoken words, there would be greater understanding and spirit of goodwill in human relationships. Just as in a melody it is the interval between two notes that matters, similarly in life too it is the interval between words and actions that is of greatest significance. It is in this interval that the quality of one's being can be perceived. To hear the melody is, therefore, to comprehend the quality of men and things. *Light on the Path* asks us to store in our memory the melody that we hear. It obviously means that we must not lose sight of the quality of men and things that we have perceived in the 'interval'. As in the interval we perceive things as they are, in their intrinsic and original nature, the memory of this perception is doubtless a memory of facts — and not the memory of projections. If the mind projects anything into the interval, then the interval ceases to be an interval.

This profound book of Mysticism asks the

neophyte to learn the lesson of harmony from the melody he has heard. Now, we have seen that melody is a succession of single notes and harmony is a succession of simultaneous or combined notes. In harmony, therefore, it is relationship — or adjustment of parts — that is of fundamental importance. When simultaneous notes are struck each part must be perfectly related to the others or else there will be disharmony and discord.

Now, for the perfect relationship of the parts, it is the memory of facts that is of supreme importance. Human relationships become unhappy and complicated when they are based on the memory of projections instead of on the memory of facts. The memory of facts is rooted in the perception of the whole. If there is no right perception, right memory is impossible, and right perception implies seeing things as they are — it is seeing the whole. To know the quality of one's being is indeed to know the whole. While a quantitative approach implies an examination of the parts, it is the qualitative approach which signifies the perception of the whole.

The quality or wholeness of a thing is perceived, not in action, not in what is manifested, but in the interval between two actions. It is in the pause — a natural pause, and not a calculated one — between actions that quality or wholeness can be comprehended. *Light on the Path* says: 'The pause of the soul is a moment of wonder.' In the pause or interval between words and actions there comes the exquisitely wonderful vision of the whole. And when the whole is perceived, the adjustment or the relationship of the parts becomes easy and effortless. In the background of the whole the pattern of relationship, in which the parts are brought together, displays a beautiful harmony. The lesson of harmony can be learned only when melody is heard. The parts which constitute the details of our everyday existence can be put in their rightful places only when the whole is perceived. The pattern of Karma presents a great puzzle and an intricate problem to us because we fail to discover the rightful place into which each detail of our life must go. To put every detail in the rightful place is indeed the lesson of harmony.

The mystery of the Part can be solved only when the Whole is perceived. It is to this perception of the Whole that *Light on the Path* leads us in the aphorisms that follow.

7

The Whisper of the Soul

The entire problem of man's spiritual life centres round two themes — the vision of the whole, and the right adjustment of the parts. The daily struggle of man is in the direction of finding a rightful place for every detail of his existence. This truly is the problem of choice, the problem of good and evil. For that which is in its rightful place is good and that which is not in its rightful place is evil. But how can one know the rightful place of anything save in the background of the whole? Without the perception of the whole the only method that man can employ for the adjustment of parts is the method of trial and error. This is an endless process especially because the psychological setting of man constantly changes. What is right in one setting may not be right at all in a changed setting. Thus, in the psychological sphere there can be no established code, no set formula, indicating what is right and wrong in an absolute manner, that is, in a manner that could be applied to all circumstances. There has to be a constant perception of the Whole. In every setting the whole has to be discovered anew.

We have already seen that the whole can be discovered only in the interval — in the silence — between two sounds. In other words, it is only as we hear the melody that we get the perception of the whole. And when the melody is heard it is easy to learn the lesson of harmony — the lesson of establishing right relationship between the parts. The question of fundamental importance in spiritual life is, therefore, that of hearing the melody — of listening to the silence, of being aware of the 'interval'. The interval holds the key to the understanding of life. The interval denotes a discontinuity. It is not continuity, but discontinuity, that reveals the meaning and significance of life!

How to listen to the silence between two sounds? The instruction which *Light on the Path* gives to the neophyte is as follows:

Regard earnestly all the life that surrounds you.
Learn to look intelligently into the hearts of men.
Regard most earnestly your own heart.

The Whisper of the Soul

We are asked to regard earnestly all the life that surrounds us, not one particular expression of life, but life wherever it expresses itself. This requires an extraordinary awareness of life at all the various levels of its expression. This is possible only under conditions of physical sensitiveness, emotional responsiveness and mental alertness. Unless a person is open and responsive in all parts of his being he will not be aware of all the life that surrounds him — and without such awareness an earnest regard for all expressions of life would become impossible. To be aware of all the life that surrounds us implies extending areas of one's own interest. Without a deep interest in life an earnest regard for its expressions is unthinkable.

Usually our interest in anything takes the shape either of identification or of condemnation. It should be noted that condemnation, too, is a form of identification — for it is an identification with the opposite of that which we condemn! If our interest in a thing, a person or an idea is born out of identification, it is only a reaction from our spheres of habit. Such a reaction may be positive or negative; in the case of condemnation we display a negative reaction. Needless to say all reactions emerge from certain fixed centres of the mind, and a fixed centre of the mind is its habit. A habit invariably dulls the mind as also the senses and thus brings a loss of perspective. An interest born out of habit can have no depth or earnestness about it. A mind conditioned by habit is lazy or indolent — it moves only within the limits of its cable-tow. Nothing outside this sphere is of any interest to it. It is quite obvious that such a mind cannot regard earnestly all the life that surrounds it. The mind that is narrowed down with reference to its sphere of interest loses a sense of proportion and thereby overemphasizes a part. It is prevented from seeing the whole by the conditioning factors of habit.

Spiritual life is essentially a piece of beautiful architecture. In such architecture there is a harmony — a sense of proportion. No part is overemphasized or underestimated. Every detail is in its appropriate place. When a part occupies its rightful place, then mysteriously the whole shines through that part. It becomes tremendously significant. In a harmonious piece of architecture every part, even the smallest detail, is significant because of the presence of the whole. When this happens there arises a natural and earnest regard for all the life that surrounds us. It is the whole which imparts significance to the part and a part becomes significant only when it occupies its appropriate place. Nowhere else can the part shine with the significance of the whole. Needless to say it is the presence of the whole which calls our undivided attention to it. It is not the size of a thing which matters. The thing by itself will remain unnoticed — it will not call out our earnest regard — if the whole is not present in it. And when the whole is present, from each detail the same quality will shine out. The difference between various things will then be only of quantity and not of quality. Thus the instruction given to the neophyte to regard earnestly all the life that surrounds him cannot be fulfilled without discovering an appropriate place for each detail of our existence. To discover an appropriate place for each detail is to have a vision of the whole. How does one come to this vision of the whole?

Here *Light on the Path* asks the neophyte to 'look intelligently into the hearts of men'. To look intelligently and to look intellectually are two different things. To look intellectually is to dissect, to analyse, to examine a thing or an event from a structural standpoint. Intellect can examine a thing only part by part — it has a static view, it splits up a movement into a number of still pictures. Intelligence, however, has a dynamic view, it can contain several things at a time, it can comprehend movement, it perceives the whole and, therefore, the appropriate place of each part.

Light on the Path says: 'Intelligence is impartial', but not so the intellect. Intellect has a personal approach to men and things, for it is the product of time. It functions from the past and into the future. It operates within the sphere of continuity, for thought is its instrument and thought is rooted in and motivated by the past. Its conclusions are based on the process of comparison and contrast. It identifies with that which evokes pleasant memories and it condemns that which stimulates unpleasant memories. And so the judgement of the intellect is personal, coloured by the memories of the past. While intellect *reacts* from the past, it is intelligence which *acts* in the present. We can look intelligently only when the judgement of the intellect is put aside. To look intelligently into the hearts of men is to see *what is*. When we see people and things as they are, we cannot help loving them. Intelligence has a direct perception, and therefore, sees the fundamental nature of everything. It sees the whole. It comprehends the source from which life's expressions emanate. The intellect only sees the outer expressions, that which is manifested. But intelligence looks into the very source and, therefore, its judgement is based on the perception of the whole. To look intelligently into the hearts of men is to see the source of action and not merely its pattern. In the source is to be found the intrinsic nature of everything. The pattern of action may be crude or refined but the source contains the original nature of everything. Our judgement of any pattern of action is bound to be faulty so long as we have not perceived the original nature of the actor who performs the action. The original nature of the actor is his dharma. An action which emanates from this centre or source is a natural and spontaneous action. It is intelligence — not intellect — which enables us to see the original nature of everything.

How to call out this intelligence from within us so that we may be enabled to look into the hearts of men? Only the man of intelligence can tread the path. We are led to the understanding of the problem as we examine the third aphorism in this particular group, which says:

Regard most earnestly your own heart.

This instruction appears on a superficial examination to be rooted in selfishness. Is not a regard for our own heart a path of self-interest? But on a deeper examination it is found to throw great light on the problem of intelligence. What does this aphorism mean, which asks us to regard most earnestly one's heart? It asks the neophyte to be sensitive to the promptings of his own heart. We listen mostly to the mind, but never to the heart.

To listen to the heart is not to become sentimental nor does it mean an emotional or an impulsive reaction to life's environment. We can listen to the heart only when the projections and motives of thought and emotion are put away. The heart speaks only to a purified mind. Everything in its intrinsic nature is absolutely pure — only when something clings to it does impurity arise. Thus, the mind becomes impure when the residue of an incomplete action clings to it. In other words, it is psychological memory which renders a mind impure. When the corruptible mind is incorrupt then only does it become sensitive to the promptings of the heart.

The heart is indeed the seat of spiritual intuition. Intelligence is that state of human consciousness which is open and sensitive to the whisper of the spirit. One of the instructions given to the spiritual aspirant is to learn to meditate in the heart. To meditate in the heart is to be sensitive to the promptings of spiritual intuition. It is to render the mind pure and transparent. It is to this purified mind that the heart conveys its secret and in the light of this secret all things become significant. He who possesses this secret regards all life earnestly — he has profound respect for everything and everyone, for he has learned intelligently to look into the heart of all phenomena.

If, while treading the path, in the midst of one's daily avocations, one could listen to the promptings of the heart, one would never miss the way. But the promptings of the heart must be obeyed. The neophyte must 'regard most earnestly' the promptings of his own heart. In a given situation, in the solution of a problem, the heart speaks but once, and that, too, in a whisper. If the mind is insensitive to the whisper of the heart, then the spiritual pilgrim must struggle and toil in the dark, and every such movement in the dark is likely to lead him astray. To disregard the promptings of the heart and to reject the guidance of intuition is to follow the path indicated by the projections of the mind. The mind is caught up in the darkness of continuity. No fundamental spiritual transformation can arise out of its efforts. Its light is only 'darkness made visible'.

However, the light of the spirit shines ever in our midst. We shall perceive this light when the screens of the mind have been put away. When the mind's continuity is interrupted, in that interval, that moment of discontinuity, one can perceive the Light Ineffable and comprehend the mystery of its shining. If only we can listen to the promptings of the heart in the midst of our daily activities, then the treading of the Path will be an indescribable joy. How can the screens of the mind be put away so that Light Eternal may be vouchsafed to us?

8

The Three Inquiries

It is in the daily life of toil and struggle, in the routine of everyday existence, that the spiritual Path has to be trodden. The path is neither physically nor super-physically away from our day-to-day activities. So, it is here that one must listen to the promptings of the heart, the whisper of the Spirit. If this whisper becomes our guide, then we are assured of a safe journey across the perilous route. However, if we fail to see 'His slightest signal across the heads of the throng', then we are sure to miss the way, for we shall then be at the mercy of the mind's projections. The neophyte has constantly to catch the orders of the Warrior in the midst of the fight. The fight cannot stop even for a moment nor can the Warrior be expected to take up arms on his behalf. He has to be a relentless fighter, and even though the fight be severe, demanding all his attention, he must yet be vigilant to see His signal and to catch His orders.

The spiritual path is indeed perilous, as sharp as the edge of a razor, and woe unto the pilgrim if sleep overtakes him even for a moment. Such are the intricacies of the path that one has to check on one's direction constantly. While checking the direction the promptings of the heart are of essential value. If the direction is not checked constantly, the neophyte is likely to miss his way and drift away into the by-paths. It is this which is indicated in *Light on the Path* towards the close of the book. It says:

The Path is found; make yourself ready to tread it.

To make oneself ready to tread the path is to hear the promptings of the heart, it is to 'regard most earnestly' one's own heart. But the question is: How to walk on the path? Is there a special technique the learning of which may enable the neophyte to walk on the path?

One needs to remember that in spiritual matters, as also in others, the question 'How' is not half as important as the questions 'What' and 'Why'. It is the latter two questions which lead a man to discovery — and once he has discovered the way, the question 'How to tread it?' becomes utterly insignificant. The way itself will tell him how to tread it! The path must be discovered by the man himself. In spiritual life the neophyte must clearly learn one lesson, and that is to know that the *word* is not the *thing*. Just because he knows the word he has not discovered the thing represented by the word. The word is only a symbol. One must comprehend that which is conveyed by the symbol. But the comprehension is not by calling out more word-pictures — it is by discovering that which is symbolized by the word. A discovery is always a direct or an unveiled perception.

If the path has been discovered by the neophyte himself then walking on it will not constitute a difficult problem to him. How to walk on the path is a secret which each man has to find out for himself. There can be no set pattern of walking on the path. A guru, a book, a discourse, can only give general directions. Just as: 'How to swim?' is a question to which an answer can be given only by plunging into water, similarly, an answer to the question, 'How to tread the path?' can be known only by actually treading the path. *Light on the Path*, therefore, gives just a few hints for the treading of the path. These hints are like signposts; they are fingers pointing the way. To regard them as more than signposts is to be utterly deluded. What are the signposts given in *Light on the Path* with regard to treading the way? They are three in number and are as follows:

Inquire of the earth, the air and the water of the secrets they hold for you.

Inquire of the Holy Ones of the earth of the secrets they hold for you.

Inquire of the inmost, the One, of its final secret which it holds for you through the ages.

Why is the neophyte asked to make these inquiries? How will these inquiries reveal the secret of treading the path? The neophyte is asked to 'inquire of the earth, air and water of the secrets they hold' for him. Now earth, air and water represent the material world. Earth, water and air are the three states of physical matter — solid, liquid and gaseous. And so, the spiritual pilgrim is required first to inquire of the material world of the secret it holds for him.

An inquiry is possible only when the neophyte is thoroughly objective — neither identifying with nor condemning the subject of inquiry. In order to engage in such an inquiry all the personal reactions of the inquirer must cease. How are these reactions

The Three Inquiries

to cease? Only as the neophyte observes his reactions, even the subtlest, to the impacts of the material world will they cease. Let him not make a conscious effort to alter them. Such effort will result only in a modification of reactions. By merely modifying one's reactions to the material environment one cannot find the secret that the earth, air and water hold for one. The very centre of reaction must break up so that there is no fixed point of the mind from where responses emanate. As long as the mind reacts from certain fixed centres, objective or impersonal inquiry must remain non-existent.

In order to break up the centres of reaction, the neophyte must observe the entire process of reactions — how they arise and why they arise. He must find out how much he is attached to material things — the phenomena of the physical world — how much material success, fame, position, possessions hold him; what are the values he attaches to these things. In other words, he must observe his reactions, even the subtlest, and see to what grade of significance he puts the material things of life. To find out the proper grade of significance with reference to material things is to know the secret which earth, water and air hold for man.

Then the book asks the neophyte to inquire from the Holy Ones of the earth as to the secret they hold for him. This inquiry is obviously directed to the psychic or the super-physical world even as the first inquiry was directed to the physical or the material world. The Holy Ones of the earth are those that possess super-physical powers. This inquiry is, therefore, to find out how much the neophyte craves for psychic powers, what value he attaches to them. There lurks in the neophyte an unconscious desire for and attachment to super-physical powers and attainments. He is likely to impart to invisible things greater importance than is due to them. The possession of super-physical powers gives to man a sense of pride, a sense of superiority. And so to inquire of the Holy Ones of the earth is to watch one's reactions to psychic phenomena and to super-physical powers. To know the secret which they hold for man is to find out their proper grade of significance. Even when a man has conquered his desires for material possessions, there remains in him the desire for psychic possessions. If such a desire lurks in the mind of the neophyte then must his movement on the path be greatly hampered.

The Three Inquiries

Light on the Path says: 'Great ones fall back even from the threshold.' To inquire of the Holy Ones is to prevent this falling back due to attachment to psychic phenomena.

It is quite obvious that in treading the path we shall stop where our attachments are fixed. Some may stop at material attractions, others at psychic attractions. The person who does not stop at either of these attractions will be ready to receive the final secret. It is to such a pilgrim that the following instruction is addressed:

Inquire of the inmost, the One, of its final secret which it holds for you through the ages.

If the inmost holds the final secret, then it is obvious that the other two — the material and the psychic worlds — have only temporary secrets; they convey only fleeting values. If we can inquire, without justification or condemnation, into the secrets of the material and the psychic worlds, if we can comprehend their grades of significance, then shall we be ready to receive the final secret from the inmost, the One.

How to inquire of the inmost the secret which it has been holding through the ages? When we see the false as false, then the Truth will be revealed to us. But seeing the false as false must be a process of direct perception by us. To declare something as false on hearsay or on the authority of others is to be deluded. On this point the instruction of the Lord Buddha is very precise:

> Do not go merely by hearsay or tradition, by what has been handed down from olden times, by rumour, by mere reasoning and logical deduction, by outward appearances, by cherished opinions and speculations, by mere possibilities, and do not believe merely because I am your Master. But when you yourselves have seen that a thing is evil and leads to harm and suffering then you should reject it.

And so, the neophyte must see for himself the false as false, and when he does that he will be able to see the true and the real. If we can realize — discover for ourselves — the falseness of material and psychic values, we shall be ready to receive the final secret. But to see the false as false has to be a constant process; otherwise there is a danger of falling even from the threshold. To see the false as false is a process in which discrimination and desirelessness are displayed as a joint phenomenon. It is this joint phenomenon of discrimination and desirelessness which truly is awareness. So long as the mind is moved on by desires, there can be no awareness, and desires will drop away only when the false is seen as false. The seeing and the dropping away of the false are a simultaneous process. There is no interval between the two. If there is an interval between seeing and dropping, then the false will reappear in a new form demanding the attention of the neophyte. It is in the simultaneous process of discrimination and desirelessness — in the moment of awareness — that the final secret will be communicated.

What is meant by a final secret? Is it fixed and static so that once communicated the neophyte can hold on to it adjusting his life in accordance with it? It cannot be, for a static concept of a final secret is utterly incompatible with the flowing, the dynamic nature of life. The finality of the secret is with reference to each situation. Paradoxically, the final secret is to be discovered from moment to moment as each moment brings a new psychological setting. To know the final secret is to comprehend what right action is at each moment. The inmost, the One, will reveal to us this secret as we inquire from it, and in the light of this secret we shall be enabled to perceive what right action is with reference to a problem or a situation.

The three inquiries indicated in these aphorisms are with reference to physical, psychic and spiritual realms. Instructed as to the final secret the neophyte can now safely tread the path, for no danger will ensue. The final secret will enable him to walk on the path with humble confidence. There is a confidence in him because the final secret has been conveyed, but there is a humility, too, for he knows that he may lose the vision if he moves away from the point of awareness. It is the razor's edge which makes the neophyte humble, but the confidence to walk on this razor-edged path has been gained by him because of the final secret having been conveyed to him.

Verily it is true that he who has comprehended the final secret walks on the Path with humble confidence. In the aphorisms that follow we are enabled to understand the implications of humble confidence with reference to the treading of the Path.

9

The Middle Way

Man is ever in search of the meaning and significance of life. A mere drifting in the current of life does not satisfy him. He seeks to assert his personal will and thereby comes into conflict with the will of Nature or the Cosmic Will. But this conflict too tires him; it keeps him chained to the process of continuity which the mind of man zealously guards. When submission and resistance to the will of Nature fail him, a pause comes in the life of the human individual. His real inquiry into the problem of life then begins. He wants to understand the meaning and the significance of the entire life-process. He is eager to know the secret that the world may be holding for him. Then begins the period of storm and aloneness. He sees in front of him nothing but utter darkness. Finding no way of escape and seeing no alternative, he stands still facing the great unknown. In this stillness or surrender he discovers the path. He is filled with a new vision and is now ready to tread the path that he has discovered.

In treading the path he finds it necessary to check his direction constantly, for the sea of life is uncharted and such are the subtle attractions of the physical and the psychic worlds that he feels he will miss his way again and again. The treading of the path demands a mastery of technique and a vision of the direction. The mastery of technique requires a positive effort but the vision of direction needs utter negativity. Thus, the negative and the positive must co-exist; action and inaction must mysteriously remain together. The neophyte must know the distinction between the Fighter and the Warrior and be ready to play the role of a Fighter carrying out the orders of the Warrior. In treading the path he must know the right relationship between the various parts of his subjective and objective environment. The parts cannot be perfectly related so long as the whole has not been comprehended. The neophyte must, therefore, listen to the melody of life and from it learn the lesson of harmony. Success on the path depends entirely upon the harmony or perfect relationship between the parts. To establish harmony is to know what right action is in the midst of ever-changing psychological settings. And it is only as man listens to the promptings of his heart, as he responds to the whisper of the Soul, that he perceives what right action is from moment to moment.

But the neophyte will be able to listen to the promptings of the heart only if he is not distracted hither and thither by the subtle cravings of the mind. If the attractions of the physical and psychic worlds detain him on the path, then he will once again be carried away into the by-paths. He will lose his direction and be subjected to a fall even from the threshold. He cannot run away from the things and the events of the physical and psychic worlds; in fact he has to tread the path amidst the din and noise of these two worlds. If he knows the grades of significance of things and events of these two realms, he will remain pure and uncontaminated. Living in the world he will not be of it, even as the lotus leaf remains unaffected by the water in which it exists. To such a pure and uncontaminated mind will come the promptings of the heart conveying the final secret as to the meaning and significance of life.

The foregoing aphorisms have revealed to man one precious truth, and that is, that only in the unchanging background of discovery can man tread the path. If the background of discovery is absent, even for one moment, then the neophyte will lose his way and be carried away by the seductions of the physical and psychic worlds.

What does the maintenance of an unchanging background of discovery mean? What is its implication with reference to the treading of the path? The three aphorisms discussed in the last chapter indicate this unchanging background of discovery. To maintain a background of discovery is to be in a state of constant inquiry — a condition of openness. The state of inquiry vanishes when a man gives undue importance to things and happenings of the physical and the psychic worlds. Undue importance implies a process either of identification or of condemnation. When due importance is given to the events and incidents of these two realms then alone can the final secret of the treading of the path be conveyed to the spiritual pilgrim.

What is meant by due importance and what is the correct grade of significance? There is a significance or importance projected by the mind. This surely is not what is meant by due importance of things and events. It is only when the mind's projected significance is regarded as real significance that man is caught up in an illusion. To be free from illusion is not to reject the world but to understand its due or real significance. To understand the real significance of things and events is to see them as they are, in perfect objectivity and not as distorted by the mind. If the spiritual pilgrim sees things and events as they are, then will he fashion appropriate patterns of action and behaviour for each moment.

The question is: In the rush and hurry of everyday life will it be possible for us to evolve appropriate patterns of action? Will not the fashioning of appropriate patterns interrupt the very process of living? It is possible to evolve appropriate patterns of action provided the mind is pliable, sensitive, ready to take whatever shape the life-impulse wants it to take. And the mind will remain pliable so long as its inquiry into the 'What' and the 'Why' of physical and psychic values continues. With reference to all events and happenings of the physical and the psychic worlds if the neophyte inquires *what* values he has put and *why* he has put those values, then the mind will have no time to settle down at any fixed point. It is in constantly challenging the values arrived at by the mind that there will arise a sensitiveness to comprehend things as they are. To comprehend things as they are is to discover the intrinsic and due value of each thing. Out of such perception of values will come a natural and a spontaneous fashioning of such patterns of action as will be most appropriate. In fact to endeavour to fashion appropriate forms without comprehending real and intrinsic values of things and events will be utterly meaningless.

To know the intrinsic values of things and events is to have a sense of proportion. In giving false values to material and psychic phenomena man loses a sense of proportion. To have a sense of proportion each moment is to know the final secret. Only with a sense of proportion can one tread the path. This is humble confidence, about which a reference was made in the last chapter. Usually in dealing with physical and psychic matters we display either the vulgarity arising out of overconfidence or the timidity born of doubt and ignorance. To avoid the rashness of vulgarity on the one hand and timidity on the other is to maintain a perfect sense of proportion.

A man of spirituality is one who has a perfect sense of proportion, a sense of right perspective.

The Middle Way

He neither overemphasizes nor underestimates the value of anything. He perceives the right values of all things because he is well poised. He is — what the *Bhagavadgitā* describes as *yukta* — balanced or harmonized. It is when the mind is well poised that there is perfect pliability — a readiness to take whatever shape the life-impulse desires it to take. Such pliability is the ground from which appropriate patterns of action are born.

This poise of the mind is difficult to maintain. When one tries to maintain it, one has already lost it! When one does not maintain it then too one has lost it! A poised mind is so delicately balanced that it demands a sleepless vigilance on the part of the neophyte. There is a very thin line of demarcation between the proper and the improper. What may be proper at one time may seem utterly improper on another occasion. So no model or ideal can be created out of the proper. The proper has to be discovered each time. A sense of proportion is not something which can be formulated in advance. It is not a pattern of action — it is the source of action. The source is so intangible that when one feels that one has caught it, it has already slipped away!

The condition of poise is most uncomfortable

for the mind, for here it finds no foothold where it can stand. It is because of this that the mind invariably jumps from one extreme to the other. It is easy for the mind to follow the path of extremes.

The two extremes of the mind are habit and ideal. Habit is the way of indulgence, of doing what one is accustomed to doing; while ideal is the path of denial, sometimes even of mortification. In pursuing an ideal the mind has to move away from its accustomed habits. It has to practice denial *now* so that it may achieve its end in the future. Indulgence and denial are the two extremes which the mind follows. It does not know what it is to be poised between these two extremes, for it finds no space between indulgence and denial where it can establish its habitat. If it refrains from habit it enters the sphere of denial, and if it refrains from denial it moves along the path of indulgence. There is a very thin line which demarcates the spheres of indulgence and denial. In fact it is a line which has length but no breadth. It is obvious that such a line cannot be defined, its position cannot be described, for to define it is to impart to it an attribute of breadth; and the moment breadth is imparted to this line,

The Middle Way

the two extremes come into existence. The mind is perpetually caught in a play of the opposites. It finds no space at all between the two extremes where it can stand and meet the challenges of life. To the mind caught in the process of opposites, to stand between the two extremes seems utterly impracticable. The practical course for it is to jump from extreme to extreme so that if indulgence is to cease, it must take its stand on the bank of denial.

One of the commonest traits of the mind with reference to human relationships is to move between the points of indifference and interference. It does not know what pure interest is, for if it is interested in anything, it interferes with its freedom, and if it is not allowed to interfere then it becomes utterly indifferent to it. The mind knows only identification and condemnation. There is no midpoint between the two which it can visualize. Pure interest, where neither identification nor condemnation, neither interference nor indifference operates — it is this which constitutes objective inquiry. It reveals the appropriate grade of significance of everything. Pure interest is a condition of poise, of balance, of harmony. To be poised is to stand where no space exists for the mind to see. It is this state of poise which *Light on the Path* indicates in the last three aphorisms which are as follows:

> *Hold fast to that which has neither substance nor existence.*
>
> *Listen only to the voice which is soundless.*
>
> *Look only on that which is invisible alike to the inner and the outer sense.*

Existence is that which is manifested; it refers to something that is concrete. While substance is the idea, the archetype, it refers to that which is abstract. The first of these aphorisms, therefore, says: 'Hold neither to the thing nor to the idea of the thing'. What is there to hold if both the concrete as well as the abstract are put aside? The mind cannot visualize any state which is neither concrete nor abstract. It is like asking it to stand where no space exists. The concrete and the abstract are indeed the two extremes — the mind jumps from one to the other.

What does holding fast to that which is neither concrete nor abstract mean? It is explained in the next aphorism which says: 'Listen to the Voice which is soundless.' As has already been discussed in the earlier part of the book, this refers to the awareness of the interval that exists between two sounds. By being aware of this interval we shall discover the point of balance, the point of perfect poise.

This idea is further explained in the third and the last aphorism which says: 'Look only on that which is invisible alike to the inner and the outer sense.' It is sometimes believed that man will discover the point of poise by transferring his attention from the visible to the invisible planes. However, the point of balance is not on the invisible planes any more than on the visible. It is not by developing clairvoyance or clairaudience that man can come to spiritual insight. The aphorism very clearly states that one has to look on that which is invisible both to the outer as well as the inner sense! The neophyte is asked to look at that which is visible neither to the sense nor to the mind. It is *that* which the mind cannot comprehend. Not in the realms of the mind can the secret of treading the path be understood.

The mind knows only the path of extremes. If the concrete is denied, then it clings to the abstract; if the visible is to be rejected it holds fast to the invisible. It is the movement to the opposites which leads a man away from the Path. It is on the Middle

Path that man can walk with firm but humble steps. It is the treading of the Middle Path which is the final secret conveyed to the neophyte by the 'inmost, the One'.

Needless to say, the middle path is not a compromise between the two extremes. The poise is not arrived at by taking a little from either of the extremes. The Lord Buddha exhorted the spiritual pilgrim to 'avoid the extremes' — but to avoid the extremes is not to have a little of indulgence and a little of denial. That would mean treading the path of comfort and convenience. The path of compromise means jumping from one extreme to the other — it means moving along the line of opposites. To walk on the middle path is to live in the intangible present. This is not the chronological, but the psychological present. This indeed is the Eternal. To live in the psychological present is to live in the Eternal Now. The Eternal is not to be confused with the everlasting. The everlasting is an infinite extension in time, but the Eternal is timeless. The Eternal is where time is not. Time comes to a stop in the present — not in the chronological present, but in the psychological present.

To be poised, balanced or harmonized is to live

in the present. The present is not a compromise between the past and the future. The past and the future belong to the process of time, but the present is timeless. It is a dimension other than where past and future function. To walk on the middle path is to be poised in the moment which is the present. When the present becomes the source of all actions, then the pattern which emerges is perfectly balanced and harmonized with every part occupying its rightful place.

To walk on the middle path is to find the final secret from moment to moment. It is final because it unlocks the mystery of life from moment to moment. On the middle path alone the great miracle takes place, the miracle of a mind holding fast to that which has neither existence nor substance. On this path the mind is free from all psychological commitments, from the pulls of the past and the future. It is only a free mind that can tread the path, for it alone can become an instrument for the expression of the life-impulse.

To live in the present — this indeed is the secret of treading the Path. It is here that the spiritual pilgrim realizes that the discovery of the Path and the treading of the Path are a joint phenomenon — not separated by an interval of time. When the discovery and the treading of the Path become a joint phenomenon then the problem of discipline no longer exists. In fact man becomes the meeting place of the great spiritual paradox: Freedom in Discipline.

About the Author

ROHIT MEHTA (1908–95) was educated in Bombay, Surat and Ahmedabad. As a student he took part in the Indian Freedom Struggle and was imprisoned on more than one occasion. He was attracted by the Socialist movement, but not being satisfied with its philosophy, he joined the Theosophical Society, soon becoming an active worker. He was the International Secretary of the Theosophical Society from 1941 to 1944, and the General Secretary of the Indian Section from 1945 to 1959.

A well-known author and eloquent speaker, Rohit Mehta travelled widely and lectured in many countries on Religion, Philosophy, Psychology, Yoga and allied subjects.

For information on
Theosophy and the Theosophical Society
please read on

Theosophy and
The Theosophical Society

The Theosophical Society, founded in 1875, is a worldwide body whose primary object is Universal Brotherhood based on the realization that life, in all its diverse forms, human and non-human, is indivisibly One. The Society imposes no belief on its members, who are united by a common search for truth and the desire to learn the meaning and purpose of existence by engaging themselves in study, reflection, purity of life and loving service.

Theosophy is the wisdom underlying all religions when they are stripped of accretions and superstitions. It offers a philosophy which renders life intelligible and demonstrates that justice and love guide the cosmos. Its teachings contribute to the unfolding of the latent spiritual nature in the human being, without dependence or fear.

For general information, contact:

International Secretary
The Theosophical Society
Adyar, Chennai 600020, India
Tel: (+91-44) 2491-2474; Fax: 2490-2706
E-mail: theossoc@dataone.in
Website: http://www.ts-adyar.org

For catalogue, enquiries, and to order books and magazines, contact:

The Theosophical Publishing House
Adyar, Chennai 600 020, India
Tel: (+91-44) 2491-1338 & 2446-6613
Fax: (+91-44) 2490-1399
E-mail: tphindia@gmail.com
    tphindia@dataone.in
Website: http://www.ts-adyar.org/catalogue.asp